Table of Contents

Introduction

Hello! Congratulations on taking a step in the direction of getting your finances under control. If you are living paycheck to paycheck and can't figure out how to get out of that rut, I think this book can help you. Let me tell you why. I've been a licensed attorney since 1999 and since that time, I've practiced in several different areas of the law. As of 2015, I've done consumer bankruptcy work for a total of 12 years. That means I filed bankruptcies for regular people, like you and me (and yes, I consider myself a regular person, I shop at Walmart just like the rest of the 99%, thank you very much). In 2014, the population of the United States was approximately 319 million. According to the United States Federal Court System, in 2014 there were 929,130 Chapter 7s and Chapter 13s filed.[1] That's nearly 1 million bankruptcies, a pretty big number, right? I filed more than a few of those cases, myself. This boils down to more than a decade of my time spent watching how people manage their money and seeing

[1] December 31, 2014, http://www.uscourts.gov/statistics-reports/caseload-statistics-data-tables

what finally drives them to file bankruptcy. So, the end result is, I know why people file bankruptcy and therefore, how it can be avoided. Eventually, I decided it was high time for me to write down the basics of money management that I believe are necessary to not just avoid bankruptcy, but to truly get your finances under control.

Thanks to my experience as a bankruptcy attorney, there are a few things I have come to realize over the years about people and money. First, most people don't have the time, or just won't read a big, old, dry and boring book about personal finance. This book is designed to be short and to the point with as many jokes crammed into it as possible, (it's hard to make jokes about a dry subject like personal finance or money stuff, but I tried my best). I've included just the basics that worked for me and some of my more dedicated clients. These are things that if many of my clients had been doing all along, they might not have needed to file for bankruptcy (not in every case, of course).

I've also tried to make it simple. I think one of the reasons people quit most financial management programs is because they use language that is too hard to understand or it's too complicated, or whatever. I try to be as simple and straightforward as possible and again, short and sweet is where it's at!

Second, having spent 12 years filing bankruptcies for regular people, I've realized the common denominator is the behavior that we as people can't seem to avoid when it comes to money. No one, and I mean absolutely no one, is above making huge money mistakes. Trust me (you can you know, I *am* an attorney after all), I've done bankruptcy consultations for other lawyers, doctors, and all kinds of professionals and even people in the financial services industry. Bad money management doesn't make you a criminal or a sinner, it makes you human! So, stop beating yourself up. The past is done. The goal is to try to improve your future.

A word or two about the jokes. Okay, some of them are really bad, I already know that. I still include jokes because I believe that any time you can laugh about something bad or uncomfortable, you take the sting out of it. Well, maybe not a paper cut on your eyeball or an attack from a swarm of killer bees, but it works for lots of other really serious topics. (See, I told you some of the jokes were bad!) We take our money—the getting it, the keeping it and the protecting it, so very seriously. It is, after all, one of the main motives for murder and crime in general. Not to mention heart attacks and all the other horrible health conditions that come from having too much stress when you don't have enough money to survive. Another reason I make a lot of jokes is that I've spent my whole professional life being serious because it was necessary and appropriate. Now it's time for me to laugh and so, I hope you do, too.

Finally, I think it's important to give you a heads up about the style of this book. If you are expecting a manual or "how to" with bullet points, calendars and diagrams, this book will definitely surprise you. It has been my experience that when you are tackling a topic that isn't a lot of fun, like money management or weight loss, the best approach is to start by helping people understand the reasons behind a course of action. Once they understand the underlying reasoning, they are far more likely to commit to a course of action, or at least finish reading the book. A dry list of "Dos and Don'ts" just doesn't seem to inspire or motivate folks to take action and frankly, it's just boring! Hopefully, the conversational nature of this book will make things a little more fun and inspiring.

Okay, it's time to get this party started. So, put your comfy that the way to cure the problem instead of just putting a band-aid on it, was to get to them before they found themselves in a spot where they had to file for bankruptcy. So, I wrote the blog with these rules, the bare minimum, for getting your personal finances under control and keeping you out of financial trouble.

For most people who find that they have to file bankruptcy, there's been some kind of life changing event. A life-changing event can be a catastrophic illness or accident, the loss of a job, the death of a spouse, a divorce or any major event that you obviously can't control. Now, bankruptcy can be a valuable tool to help you manage those life-changing events. That is absolutely true and if you need to file for bankruptcy, say for example your credit card debt totals more than one third of your gross annual salary, you should talk to a qualified bankruptcy attorney in your state to help you with that process. However, you ***can*** manage your finances in a way that will help you keep from living paycheck-to-paycheck, or worse, having to file bankruptcy. If you are following my rules, you could probably even survive a life-changing event. So, what are the rules? Here you go!

Rule 1: Live within your means. This idea really should

explain itself. The best way to achieve this goal is to set a budget and stick to it. When I meet with clients the first time, I ask them to bring their income information, a list of their assets and a list of their debts. I have estimated that about 80% of my clients have never done a budget. They only have a general idea of how much money is coming in and how much money is going out. A majority of them only have a general idea of how much debt they have, too. When I start trying to pin them down on figures, they have to "get back to (me) on that." They usually do know how often they get paid and how much money their pay check is, almost to the penny. That's my first clue that they are living paycheck-to-paycheck. Here's a newsflash, ***if you file for bankruptcy the law REQUIRES YOU TO DO A BUDGET AND INCLUDE EVERY DEBT[2]. On top of including an income and expense document, you also are REQUIRED by law to take a credit counseling class before filing. You have to file a certificate stating you completed the credit counseling class with the bankruptcy petition!*** Did you get that message? Budgeting is extra, super, double important!

---

[2] A standard bankruptcy petition requires you to complete Schedule I and Schedule J, which are your income and expense schedules, respectively. You are also required to complete form 22, which is essentially a budget based on national standards for living expenses.

Chances are pretty good that if you are budgeting as a habit, you won't have to worry about filing bankruptcy! This rule also means you need to keep it real. If you are making $30,000 a year, you should not be living in a home with a $400,000 mortgage on it. Again, the budget is the key.

There's a whole chapter later in the book about budgeting! (Yay, let the good times roll!!) I won't get into specifics here but, budgeting allows you to make sure you pay yourself first by creating a spending plan (a fancy phrase that means, well ... a budget), that includes saving, or investing, a percentage of your income off the top. It starts with keeping track of every penny for 30 days (this is called 30-day expense tracking). Then, with that information, begin to look for ways you can shave down expenses and spend more carefully. Learning to budget can be painful at first but it's a skill that is worth its weight in gold and will last a lifetime. If you are paying yourself first, you'll be less likely to miss the money. Learn how to budget and practice budgeting daily. Budgeting is an investment in you and the most important investment you can make!

Here's a little something to think about, you should even

budget if you have a surplus of money. The following statistics help explain the importance of budgeting and managing money for everyone. According to a paper issued in April of 2015 from the National Bureau of Economic Research, financial problems among NFL players start just after retirement. In fact, most NFL players who file for bankruptcy do so in the twelve years after retirement. (NBER Working Paper No. 21085, April, 2015.) Everyone should be learning how to budget and live within their means!

Rule 2: Don't keep getting into debt. Again, this idea should explain itself, but it seems that I find myself repeating this rule again and again. Here is a rule of thumb that I have always used in my bankruptcy practice, if your total UNSECURED debt (that means credit cards, medical bills, personal loans and etc.), is one third or more of your gross annual salary, it could take decades for you to pay it off, if you make only the minimum payment(s) every month. Depending on the interest rate, it could take 20 years or more, and you'll wind up paying a whole lot more than the original amount, too. Be really honest about what you need versus what you want. If you can't pay for it with cash, don't buy it unless it's an absolutely necessity. See the NCV.com 4 Question Flow Chart included at the

previous interest payments. Hot dignity dog!! I love compound interest! I sum it up like this, people should be paying you interest, not the other way around.

Now, here's a quick guide about how to determine how much of your income to save. Take your paystubs (or list out your monthly income deposits if you don't get a paycheck—if you get Social Security payments, for example), and add up your income BEFORE DEDUCTIONS, every month. That is your GROSS monthly income. If you add it up AFTER DEDUCTIONS, that is your NET monthly income. Now, you should be saving a percentage of your GROSS income. Not your NET.

Just in case you are as bad at math as I am (shh, don't tell anyone you know a bankruptcy attorney who is bad at math), you figure out the percentage of your income by taking the gross amount and multiplying it by the percentage amount you are looking for. So, if you make $36,000 a year and you are looking for 3% of that amount, get your calculator and multiply 36,000 by .03. Your answer should be 1,080. If you are looking for 15%, you should multiply 36,000 by .15. Your answer should be 5,400. Get it? So, let's break that down a little more. If your monthly amount is

$1,080 (that's 3% of your annual $36,000 gross amount), and you divide that amount by 12, you get $90 a month that you need to save in order to save 3% of your gross salary. That is $22.50 a week or just $3.21 a day. What a bargain, yay!!

Look at it this way, that daily cup of coffee from that store we won't name (but it begins with an "S" and ironically has the word "bucks" in it), could be brewing away your nest egg. Now, if you save the recommended minimum of 15%, your goal is only $16.07 a day. You could probably save most of that amount by, and here comes the biggest hole in the ground that Americans throw money into, ***<u>NOT EATING OUT</u>***. According to Trent Hamm who wrote *The Simple Dollar*, the average American spends $232 a month eating out, which works out to about three meals a week.[3] In my experience, that $232 is a low estimate. I've told bankruptcy clients that I rarely eat out and they look at me like I've got two heads. That's a shame because a future of financial independence is certainly worth learning how to make spaghetti and meatballs, don't you think?

Rule 4: Invest your money. Don't just save 15% of your

---

[3]July 31, 2014, http://www.thesimpledollar.com/dont-eat-out-as-often-188365/

income, invest it. Stashing money into a savings account earning less than 1% in interest is little better than stuffing the money into your mattress. You need to put it in an account where it can work for you and earn interest. Remember my rule, people should be paying you interest not the other way around. I suggest a no load (meaning minimal management fees), Roth IRA (Individual Retirement Account), to start with. It should be a Roth IRA because your withdrawals are tax deferred after retirement! You can put up to $6,000, or $12,000 for a married couple, into a Roth IRA every year! (See, that's 17% of your income if you both earn about $36,000 a year together! Only a little more than the recommended 15%. Hocus pocus, it's almost magic!). You can also withdraw the ***money you've put in*** if you need it without penalty, because you've already paid tax on it. (A nice alternative to a savings account for an emergency fund, don't you think?). These are just a few of the benefits of a Roth IRA. ***Also, IRAs may be protected in bankruptcy or from judgment creditors (people who sue you), depending on the state you live in!!*** This means that even if you have to file bankruptcy or you get sued by a creditor, your IRA might be protected. Just make sure you are investing in *no-load* funds. Watch out for expensive management fees that can eat up 50% to 70% of the return on your investment over time. Remember my disclaimer, and this is the lawyer coming out in me, check your state's rules for bankruptcy and judgment creditor exemptions. A good bankruptcy lawyer can help you do that, if necessary.

A final word about investing. You should not be investing a significant amount of money if you are paying interest on unsecured debt, like credit cards or personal loans. The interest you would earn from the investment probably would not be enough to offset the interest you are likely paying on your credit cards. Pay those debts off as quickly as possible and then start investing. The longer you wait to invest, the more you will lose out on time and compounding on your investments. One exception to this rule is if you have an employer sponsored 401(k) with an employer match. You should invest in it immediately and enough to get the full amount of the employer match. Just make sure you pay off your high interest rate debt as quickly as possible and then start investing a consistent percentage of your gross income. Of course, you should tailor this rule to your situation. When it comes to personal finance, one size doesn't necessarily fit all.

Chapter 2 – It's all in your head

Why, you may be asking yourself, would a bankruptcy attorney include a chapter called "it's all in your head" in a book about personal finance? Some of you were probably expecting a book with percentages, statistics and laws or a "how to" book that is more like a personal finance manual. Well, if I believed that type of book would work for teaching regular people, like you and me, about money management, I would have written it that way. The truth is, before we get into the specifics about budgeting and things like that, it's important to talk about your money mindset or mentality. I have seen a direct connection between how and why we think the way we do about money and the actual state of our personal finances. You may think that's a lot of baloney but, it's really not. I'll explain more about that shortly.

Over the years, I've read a lot of books, blogs, magazines, websites and all sorts of things on personal finance. Some of them hint at the importance of our money mindset but very few of them really get into it. I haven't see a whole lot of information out there about why we think the way we do about money and I believe that's because any time you talk about anything that's emotional or introspective, people start to look at you like you are a kook. Well, I'm hoping that the fact that I'm a licensed, bankruptcy attorney will lend some street cred to what I'm about to say. So here goes ...

I know for a fact that financial security is a state of mind. Hear me out, scoffers! Remember, I've been a practicing attorney since 1999. Between 1999 and 2015, I've practiced consumer bankruptcy law for a combined total of 12 years. During that time, I've spoken to thousands of people about their financial situations. Over the years, and through countless conversations, I've come to realize that many of the people I've talked to had the same spending patterns and general behavior, or a behavioral common denominator. This goes for people who filed bankruptcy and for people who didn't. I've even recognized that behavior in myself in years past and you know what they say, hindsight is 20/20!

Again, it's important to remember that I've done bankruptcy consultations for other professionals including lawyers, doctors and people in the financial services industry as well as people who were store clerks, manual laborers and many who were unemployed and unemployable. I also recently read an article about an Ivy League trained economist who was making pretty big money mistakes so, like I said before, anyone can fall into a money trap. Through all of those experiences, I came to understand that most of the time, money problems start with a person's mentality, with their mindset about money.

Please note that I'm not passing judgment, not even close. In fact, I wasn't always that great at personal finance, either. I had to learn it, just like everyone else! Unfortunately, most of us were not lucky enough to have been born Rockefellers, nice to meet you fellow members of the 99%! Financial security is hard enough to achieve when you have accountants for parents let alone when they are working day and night to feed their families with little time for anything else.

Now, let me just state for the record that I'm not saying you can think yourself rich. Not at all. What I'm saying is (to paraphrase a line that I think came from Dr. Phil McGraw), you have to behave your way to financial security. And we all know, hopefully, that behavior starts in your head. If your attitude, beliefs, perspective, relationship with, or concept of money is off or skewed, you will never, ever get it under control. You can categorize it any way you want but if you constantly make financial decisions based on your emotions or bad behavior you learned as a kid, for example, you will never develop self-control, which is critical for financial security. Having self-control really means learning how to manage your behavior. Truthfully, the most expensive thing you can do in your life is fail to learn self control.

Just in case you're still not sure about how important our money mindset is, here's a story that will help you understand the idea. In her book *9 Steps to Financial Freedom*, Suze Orman tells the story about her dad running into his burning restaurant to grab the cash register when she was 13 years old. He had already escaped the building unharmed, but he ran back inside when he realized every dime of his family's money was in the cash register. When he ran back in, he had to grab the hot metal cash register and run back out of the burning building, getting severely burned in the process. Suze saw it happen and she says the lesson she learned from that experience was that money was more important than life. I get it, what an experience for a 13-year-old. However, we should all know that mentality is absolutely wrong, money is never

components of your money mentality. Do it when it's quiet and you can really think. Also, be brutally honest. If you lie to yourself about this, you really aren't doing yourself any favors. Don't worry, you can trash or shred the list when you're done. Like wearing a Speedo, no one needs to see it but you. Just make sure you do the work. Spend some time thinking back to when you were a kid. What did you learn from your parents about managing money? Were they late paying the bills all the time? Were your parents like mine, way too busy to teach you anything about money management? Probably, or you wouldn't have purchased this book, and by the way, thanks for that!

Once you've done this homework, you can begin to work on seeing your patterns about money and changing your behaviors. You may ask yourself, why is this important? Well, changing your mindset starts with understanding your history with money. Once you understand why you think the way you do, you begin to become more aware of your thought patterns about money and then you can start to adjust your thinking in the moment. This in turn, will also help you see your current situation in a new way. A daily practice of gratitude for what you have in your life now is also invaluable in helping to readjust your mentality and perspective. In fact, gratitude is so important that I think the next couple of paragraphs may very well be the most important in this entire book.

First, I strongly encourage you to develop a practice of gratitude as part of your financial management plan. It may sound kooky but I can't tell you how important it is to help you get your finances on track. When you are thankful for what you have, even if it's only watching a video of a dog riding a bike on YouTube (you know that's funny, don't deny it), you are opening yourself to the possibility that even in hard times, you can receive abundance. That is something to be thankful for.

Second, if you can stop visualizing yourself as broke or unable to get your finances under control you are actually a lot farther along in your journey toward financial stability than you think. This idea actually goes hand in hand with your practice of gratitude. Remember, your overall attitude really does determine your altitude. As you begin to cultivate gratitude for what you do have, and to think of yourself as more and more financially secure and savvy, you will begin to be more aware and mindful of how you spend money and manage your finances. Soon, it will become easy to spot your spending patterns and anticipate problems with your budget. You start to get used to the idea of being financially savvy and then eventually it will be part of your identity and become second nature. This change in mentality will do two things: first, it will help you begin to see the value in the concept that small actions really do matter (we'll talk more about this later). Second, it will also help you realize that your value as a person has absolutely nothing to do with your finances. Always remember, YOU ARE NOT YOUR MONEY!!!

You should know by now that it takes a very long time for a behavior to become a habit so give yourself a break if you don't catch on to pattern spotting right away or if you fall off the mindfulness wagon. It happens to everyone! Try to remember that tomorrow is another day and you can try again. After all, financial security doesn't happen overnight unless you win the lottery and even then, having a boatload of money doesn't mean you are financially secure. Just ask Willie Nelson or MC Hammer!

A note about shame and fear ... Over the years, I've watched many people get themselves into financial trouble because they were terrified of facing their financial problems and then they collapse under the weight of their shame when their situation begins to unravel. First of all, shame and fear can be debilitating. They can literally reduce you to the point of inaction. I've seen people get physically ill from the shame and fear of failed personal finances. I've seen them work themselves into states where they are totally incapable of making any rational or educated choice and worst of all, I've seen it tear families apart.

When it comes to feeling shame about our finances, I always try to let people know that the best thing for them to understand is that anyone can make financial mistakes. Regardless of what caused the situation, there is no reason to be ashamed of it. The goal is to rise above it and survive it. Shame is a tough one, though. Shame is something we create in our minds and carry around with us like a bunch of hidden, extra baggage. The way to deal with it is to get it out in the open and make a plan to handle the situation. If you are up front about it and proactive about things, you can manage the shame. Also, it's important to remember anyone can make mistakes and everyone does. Money mistakes are nothing to be ashamed of. I can think of a bunch of things to be ashamed of from my past, like acid washed jeans and my 7th grade

bankruptcy … I could go on and on!

The key to controlling your fear is not avoiding it, it's understanding that fear is a natural human emotion. It's normal to feel it, you just can't let it consume you and become your identity. You need to acknowledge it, realize you are safe in the moment and then, just like the Winter Warlock in that classic childhood Christmas movie *Santa Clause is Coming to Town*, you have to keep putting one foot in front of the other and soon you'll be walking out the door! That means you need to take action in spite of your fear!

And finally, if you are in a shame spiral, stand up right this second and take a deep breath, then clap your hands three times and yell out, "I am not a jelly doughnut!" Did that make you laugh? Good! That was my intention. Money mistakes are not the end of the world, don't treat them like they are. At the end of the day, remember what the Green Lantern said about fear, "Fear is the enemy of will and will is what makes you take action. Fear is what stops you and makes you weak … you must ignore your fear. When you are afraid, you can't act, when you can't act, you can't defend and when you can't defend, you die." You GO Green

Lantern!

Chapter 3 – The Spanx Method

Now we've come to the thrilling part of this book. Learning how to budget. What in the world does that have to do with Spanx[4]? We'll get to that later in the chapter. For now, let's work on really learning how to budget. I can hear the groans from the millions of readers across the world! Yes, budgeting can be tough to learn, if you aren't wired for it. I know that it wasn't easy for me to learn but, I did it. So, if I can do it, you can, too!

Before we get started, try to figure out a way to make budgeting fun. I bet you're asking how that could be possible, like, ever. Well, you really can make it fun. For example, try wearing something special when you budget, like maybe a giant foam rubber cowboy hat, or even better, nothing at all! You can budget naked! That could be fun if you're a couple. Or, you can make a game of it by setting goals for yourself. When you hit each goal, give yourself a creative reward like sneaking into your in-law's house, putting on your mother-in-law's girdle and doing lunges for

[4] Here's a shout out to Sara Blakely and Spanx, Inc. Thank you for introducing us to the world of better living through shapewear!

20 minutes while she's at bingo night.

You see? Budgeting really can be fun! I swear! But first, you actually have to start doing it. So, let's begin. A good place to start is with the word "budget." Dictionary.com defines it as "an estimate of income and expenditure for a set period of time." Truthfully, who hasn't heard this word? Everyone! We all seem to kind of know the word even if we don't really know how to do it, right? What most people don't realize is that you can't get your finances under control and begin to build wealth without a budget. So, why do we dread the idea of budgeting? Because it takes effort, progress happens slowly, and it can be frustrating at first. There really is no secret to budgeting, or even successful money management but, if there was a secret to it, it's this ... you just have to commit to it and do it. It's true that budgeting is a lifestyle choice like losing weight. You have to enter into it consciously and mindfully, with the right intention.

Now, we know everyone has heard the word budget, but what is it really? A budget or spending plan, is a simple tool that we use to determine how much money we have coming in, what our expenses are and ultimately, how much money we have left over or, our bottom line. Okay, what in the world does that mean? Let's

probably within arm's reach right now), and put the bill payment due date in your calendar. Make sure you pay it on time!

I prefer to keep track of my stuff electronically. I get e-statements and bills and print them off as .pdf files which I keep in files on my hard drive. This cuts down on the amount of paper I have to deal with. As a lawyer, I keep way too much paper anyway. The less paper I have to keep, the better! And, no paper cuts, yee HAW!!

Now, I just mentioned one of the best tools you can use to get yourself organized and get your personal finances under control. Can you guess what it is? Your smartphone. If you guessed correctly, I'm not surprised! Practically everyone in the free world has a smartphone, these days. Even if you don't have a smartphone, ten bucks says you have a basic cell phone. The simplest cell phones have three important tools that you absolutely should be using to get, and keep, your personal finances in order. Your phone has a calendar, calculator and a notepad function. I guarantee it does, unless it's one of those ancient bag phones that Motorola manufactured back in the '80s.

These three tools can make the difference when managing

your financial situation. First and foremost, always make sure you put the due date for your bills in the calendar. Paying your bills on time can account for 1/3 of your credit score, make sure you don't pay them late if you can help it. The calculator is a no brainer. It can help you do the simple math you need when managing your money, like figuring interest and percentages, and most importantly, balancing your checkbook register. A small math mistake can have really huge consequences in your personal finances (like multiple bounced checks and late fees, etc). Small actions really do matter. Always, ALWAYS use your calculator and, if you know you are mathematically challenged, make it a habit to do each calculation three times or add then subtract your column of numbers, or something like that. Just make sure to double-check your math. It can save you a ton of grief, believe me. Anyway, the message is your phone has a calculator, use it! We'll get to the notepad feature in a minute.

You really can get as fancy, or as technical as you want with your budget. For example, there are lots of apps and websites out there designed to help you get organized and create a budget. I suggest you check them out and see which ones might work for you. Anything that helps you stay organized is worth a try, just make sure you are keeping your identity and banking information secure.

Finally, if you are still intimidated about getting organized, remember that Oprah Winfrey said she used to keep her "important papers" in a basket and look how far she's come! So get that basket and start organizing.

2. 30-day expense tracking.

This is where most people fall down because it requires daily attention. What is 30-day expense tracking? Well, for 30 days you write down every, and I mean EVERY, expense. An easy way to accomplish this task is to use the notepad function on your smart phone. Keep track of the date, expense type and how it was paid. Some expenses are easy to track from your credit card or bank website but cash expenditures can slip through the cracks, that's why the notepad is so important. If you use a spreadsheet for your budget and you are tech savvy, you can set up a separate tab for 30-day expense tracking, which is what I do (and yes, I still do a form of 30 day expense tracking even after years of managing my personal finances). You can enter your info there, sort it, add it up and plug it into your monthly budgeting spreadsheets where necessary.

You should practice 30 day expense tracking for at least three months. At the very least, you should be doing it until you get an idea about what your spending patterns are. If you just do it for 30 days and then quit, you may miss important but “unseen” expenses which could throw your budgeting way off. For example, what about seasonal expenses, quarterly homeowner’s association dues, etc.? If you do it for just a month and then quit, you are also missing out on the value of the fact that paying attention to your finances everyday helps create awareness and mindfulness in your spending. At the end of the day, the goal is to try to make budgeting a habit, a lifestyle change to help you keep your personal finances on track, long term.

Let’s talk about the elephant in the room—budgeting with your spouse or significant other. Well … that’s a tough one. Money is one of the biggest reasons people in relationships argue. A common phrase among bankruptcy attorneys is that bankruptcy law and divorce law go hand in hand. I have done bankruptcy consultations and divorce consultations back to back many times

mind.

The thing to remember is that if you are choosing to be together, you are also choosing to compromise to make that happen. Keep your main goal in mind when you see your husband spending hundreds at Home Depot but failing to pay the cable bill on time every month! Remember, no one is perfect so, always speak and act from a place of love when you are discussing money. If you are coming from a place of love, you can move mountains together!

Finally, remember Professor Randy Pausch? If you don't know who he is, you should Google him. In his "Final Lecture," he said lots of powerful things. One thing in particular, really stuck with me and that was, "never put things before people." In my opinion, that includes money. Now, I'm not saying give your money away with reckless abandon. Generosity is a great and noble thing, just be smart about it. Find a happy medium. Don't be a scrooge but don't be a spendthrift either. Don't cast your pearls before swine and don't loan money that you can't afford to lose. It's hard to help others when you yourself need to be rescued.

3. 30-day review.

Okay, you're organized and you've spent 30 days tracking your expenses, what's next? Now you need to take the information you've collected and begin to use it.

Again, you can use any number of platforms to set up your budget, but for the purpose of this book we are going to stick with low-tech pencil and paper! In fact, I have included a printable budget sheet on my website, www.newcashview.com, and as an example in Appendix E to this book. So, on your printed sheet or in your notebook, set up two columns: an income column and an expense column like the income statement graphic Figure 1 from earlier in this section. Write down all sources of income in the income column, add them up and write the total at the bottom of the column.

The second column is for your expenses. This column needs a little more organization. Start with your fixed expenses at the top. These are expenses like your mortgage, car payment, student loan payment, etc. We call them "fixed" expenses because they are generally for a fixed amount every month. Your next expenses are semi-fixed. These are more like your telephone and cable expenses, etc. Finally, take your 30-day expense tracking numbers and add them up according to category. These expenses are your "variable" expenses. We call them variable expenses because they vary every month. So, for example, look through your 30-day expense tracker and figure out how much are you spending on grocery stores. Add up all the individual charges and include the result as one figure in your expense column.

I would suggest breaking the food category out by groceries, eating out, school lunches, etc. The reason for this is that the food category is the sneakiest category. It can look like you're spending a ton of money on food but the truth is, you aren't spending money at the supermarket, you are spending it at the local pizza place, burger joint or family restaurant. Once you get all of your expenses listed, add them up and write the total at the bottom of the expense column.

Now, subtract the total amount of your expenses from the total amount of your income and what you have is your "net income." Your net income is the amount you have left over at the end of every month. If that is a positive number for you then, YAY!! If not, you have some work to do!

4. Time to plan!

So, you've done several months worth of expense tracking and have created your budget template. What's next? This is the planning stage where you look at your information and decide how to start adjusting your budget to achieve your financial goals. This is where you sit down and take a few minutes to hammer out some short-term and long-term financial goals for yourself. I suggest your short-term goals should start with your monthly expenses which leads me to the most common question I get about budgeting: how much of my budget should I be spending on housing, food, transportation, etc.?

There are all kinds of plans, programs, suggestions, formulas, algorithms, etc. that are designed to tell you how much to save and spend on every possible category. My suggestion starts with the notion that your budget is, and should be, specific to you and your goals. I call it "finding your magic number." Once you've looked at your numbers and set your goals, then you can figure out your magic number. Your magic number should satisfy all of these requirements:

— It should pay your reasonable living expenses, the things you NEED to live.

a big number. It needs to be meaningful to YOU! And that could be a smaller number than you realize! Don't forget David Bach,[6] the financial author who came up with the concept of the "latte factor." The idea is basically that small daily actions/savings/investments can turn into significant financial resources over time. Is there a small regular expense in your budget that you can channel into your savings? It bears repeating: choose a meaningful amount for YOU!

You know, thinking about ways to save money without actually knowing what you are spending is like trying to lose weight without ever having stepped on a scale. Have you ever KNOWN you've gained weight but been afraid to step on a scale to see how much? How do you know you've gained weight? Because your Spanx have gotten REALLY tight or your favorite jeans are starting to reveal more than you are comfortable with. Do you follow? You KNOW you've gained weight but you have no idea how much and so, even though you know you need to lose weight or save money, you don't know how many calories are in that seemingly low cal yogurt or how much money you REALLY spent at TJ Maxx! I call

---

[6] Accessed September 24, 2015, http://www.finishrich.com/lattefactor/

this, “The Spanx Method.” People use it for dieting AND budgeting. You know you need to cut back on the pumpkin spice lattes when your Spanx, and your bank account, are stretched so tight they're see through!

I'm sure you get my point, that your money and your weight work the same way. You KNOW you are short at the end of every month or that your husband has been spending too much time at Home Depot. You KNOW you've gone to Red Robin one too many times this month but unless you are keeping track of your numbers, you don't know HOW MUCH you are in the hole. You are basically flying blind! Don't forget, you've conquered your fear and changed your mentality, now take the next step and be proactive! Let's look at those numbers and see if we can't put some breathing room back in those Spanx!

This step helps you see what your spending priorities have been and where you are bleeding money! This step also helps you begin to develop a sense of how to prioritize your spending. Was that expensive steak dinner at that fancy restaurant really satisfying, long term? Maybe in the moment, but a pot luck or back yard barbeque shared with friends can be more satisfying in the long run, and cheaper, too! Do you really need to drive that swanky Cadillac that costs a fortune to fix when you lay awake at night worrying about money? Maybe not, you won't know for sure until you know how to budget!

Chapter 4 – Breathing room

Okay, full disclosure, this chapter is about financial philosophy. I know, I know, didn't we sort of already cover this in Chapter 2? And what does that have to do with breathing room? Well, just bear with me for a few minutes because this is really important. When I first started thinking about teaching a budgeting class, I tried to think of an analogy that would highlight the balance between the emotional pitfalls of budgeting and the importance of it, while also incorporating the concept of mindfulness and small, consistent, daily actions. In my mind, that was a no-brainer ... what's the other area of our lives that requires the same amount of self-discipline and mindfulness? I'll tell you, if you haven't already guessed it: weight loss.

For me, this analogy really drives the point home. I've actually been using this analogy for a long time, and here's why. I have a good friend who has struggled with her weight all of her life. (Haven't we all been trying to lose the same 10 lbs for years!). One day about 10 years ago, she said something to me that really hit

moment impacts you in a big way. Remember Newton's third law: for every action, there is an equal and opposite reaction. This is especially true in budgeting and weight loss. For example, when you are shopping online and thinking about whether or not to buy that pair of shoes or gadget that you really, REALLY want, even though you aren't sure you can afford it and then you buy it anyway because, "I work hard so I deserve it," right? Or, like when you are about to have that glass of wine worth four points even though you know you are about to go to dinner at your favorite restaurant with those really decadent deserts, (unless you are going to dinner at your mother in law's, then by all means, have the glass of wine, it's medicinal!).

All of those small choices you make add up. Even with little things, such as when you are about to eat that bite size Snickers out of your kid's Halloween candy. In that moment, when you are about to put it in your mouth you are thinking "mmmmm Snickers!" but you hesitate because you know you have to weigh in on Friday. Then you decide to eat it anyway because it's bite size and that's harmless! And before you know it, you've eaten 20 of those stupid things. When you weigh in at the end of the week, you will see the equal and opposite reaction. Each of those choices are going to show on the scale, just like your bank balance will show whether or not you have enough cash to pay the rent. It is inevitable and we all know that just like your Spanx, the numbers don't lie! And that, my friends, is the "The Spanx Effect," or the result of "The Spanx Method" of budgeting! When you are eating right and sticking to your budget, you will have more room to breathe in your Spanx AND your bank account! Let's say it again, all together now: the Spanx don't lie! FYI, they do make Spanx for men, too. Just throwing that out there.

Seriously, the weigh in, or reckoning, at the end of the week is really accountability. That's another great thing about the Weight Watcher's analogy; accountability is built in to their weight loss program, (just like your Spanx!). The idea is to build the same accountability into your personal finance management and that's what the profit and loss statement is for! For your purposes, keep in mind the 4 Question Flow Chart included at the end of this book. Keeping it in the back of your mind will help keep you accountable. Again, don't forget that accountability is critical and is a product of mindfulness.

Now, here's the brain twister ... accountability is a product of mindfulness, and vice versa. Think about that for a minute. Is your brain twisted yet? If you are being mindful then ultimately, you are accountable. So, the converse is also true, inherently. If you are accountable, you will also be mindful because you know an accounting is coming, (thank you Weight Watchers!). Again, this also reinforces the concept that small actions matter. If you can master the small immediate act of spending mindfully and KEEPING TRACK OF IT, you have mastered the technique of budgeting and harnessed its power!

Mindfulness really is critical to both dieting and managing your money. Mindfulness also helps you ease the pain of dieting and budgeting. It allows you to take control of your eating and spending! Think of it like this, you aren't depriving yourself when you are keeping track of points, you are simply making a choice about how you choose to eat your points. You have the power to make that choice because you are aware of the choice in the moment. This also empowers you to take small, consistent actions that will result in the cumulative goal you are aiming for. And just like Weight Watchers, small daily actions (keeping track of points) add up to big, long term results! This is important enough to repeat: if you are aware of how you are spending in the moment, you gain a powerful advantage in managing your daily personal finances that will reveal itself as you continue the practice in the months to come.

Now it's really important to be clear about something. When I say be mindful or aware in the moment, I don't mean repeating your mantra of "I can't afford this" or "I'm tired of being broke." I mean be aware of having a choice about how you spend the money you have, NOW. Remembering to change your mentality includes changing how you see yourself and your finances. It is critical for you to see yourself as someone who CAN manage money and build wealth.

Every time I think of how to teach the concept of mindfulness, I think of cheese. Remember the Laughing Cow commercial? When did eating become mindless? Stop mindlessly reaching into the potato chip bowl! Snack on small, individually wrapped cheeses to help you avoid eating mindlessly! When I saw that commercial, it stuck with me. Who hasn't mindlessly chowed down on some delicious potato chips while binge watching your favorite TV show? Yours truly is definitely guilty of that! (Whoever

lasting weight loss over a long period of time. Their program allows you to eat food you love so you don't feel deprived. The same concept or principle, applies in budgeting and money management. The idea is not to create a budget that is so tight you can't enjoy life. The idea is to design a budget that over time, allows you to make small CONSISTENT adjustments that result in the long term management of money by paying down debt, saving consistently and investing those savings smartly.

I think it's important to dig a little deeper into the concept of the importance of small actions. Just to demonstrate the value of small daily actions in your finances, remember the Latte Factor. A guy named David Bach coined the term and outlined the idea that a small daily savings, like a cup of coffee (even a $1 cup of coffee every morning from McDonald's is $250 a year), or a morning Mountain Dew or Coke (which I know some people prefer), could add up to $1 million in retirement savings over a 30 year period, give or take.

Now, a lot of people argued against it saying the math was not correct or didn't factor in changing returns on investments and etc. They might be right, but the kernel of the idea remains sound. If you buy a $2 cup of coffee or soda on your way to work every day for a year, and you work for about 200 days a year, that's $400 that you could save and contribute to your retirement savings annually. Assuming an average rate of return of 6% over 20 years, you would have $15,597.06. That is a pretty significant contribution to say, a Roth IRA—just from saving your Mountain Dew money every day. It is almost double the $8,000 you would have if you only saved the $2 a day in your mattress. See, those small expenditures really do matter!

Recently I've heard another take on the small actions savings plan based on the SMarT concept. You can Google it and see that SMarT is actually a mnemonic acronym designed to help achieve business goals. The application I've heard is that if you commit to save 3% of your income now but commit to saving 50% of any raise you get in the future, in a relatively short period of time you will be saving 15% - 20%. It'll happen before you know it! This program encourages saving a small amount now and increasing it when you get a raise or a higher paying job, etc. And, you won't feel it because you make the commitment BEFORE you get the raise!

Finally, after a period of mindful spending, look through your expenses to see which of your expenses are not serving your new mindful mentality. You will begin to develop an ability to recognize unnecessary expenses that are not serving your long-term financial plan. For example, I had a client who owned a single-family home. She was a widow and her children were long since grown and gone. She was still paying a mortgage on a house that was big enough for a family, on her substantially reduced income. During her consultation, we had a long talk about how that big mortgage payment no longer suited her needs or her budget. She made the choice to move to a beautiful, small apartment with a monthly rent payment at about half the amount of her mortgage payment. She had plenty of space and no grass to cut! Some months later, she called me and told me how relieved she was to be out from under that mortgage payment, and the worry of maintaining the property, etc.

This client adjusted her expenses to align with her new mentality and in the process, she freed up several hundred dollars a month. She was able to establish a budget that her fixed monthly income was enough to fund without a shortage every month. She did not have to consider a part time job, which she was thinking about getting when she first came to see me. She even had a little money left over every month for lunch and bingo!

Ultimately, it's important to keep in mind the reasons behind striving to achieve financial security:

1. Being able to be fully present for your family and in every moment of your daily life.
2. Peace of mind. Like Dad said, a good night's sleep starts with not having to worry about money.
3. So you have money when you need it, like when you have to pay for your children to go to college.
4. So you have money when you don't need it. The goal is not to deprive yourself; the goal is to enjoy your life NOW!
5. Having enough money changes the way you make decisions. You are no longer in the rat race and you have the ability to step back from an otherwise stressful situation and take the time to think through your options so you can make the best decision for you and your family.
6. Long term security. Maintaining your current lifestyle into retirement.

Me personally, I used to have a hard time with failure. Like the time I decided it would be fun to learn how to break dance in the 7th grade. It was a very, very unfortunate experience. It didn't take long for me to figure out that I'm really not that coordinated. The best I can do is the robot so; I'll stick to that, thank you very much! It took a long time for me to learn that failing at something is a part of life and your failures can be the most valuable experiences you can have. About my financial mistakes, I made most of them when I was just starting out and so I've been able to recover pretty quickly. The truth is, even if you are older and you made a critical money mistake, you can still begin to re-position yourself so you will not feel the consequences of your mistake so deeply over time.

There are really two aspects of failure that are important to remember. First, a result of failing is learning. That makes a lot of sense, if you think about it. It's just like that quote that seems to be everywhere these days, "no experience is wasted." I've heard that phrase a quite few times over the last several years and I believe it's true. Along those same lines, I recently read a book about building wealth that devoted a fair amount of time discussing how wealthy people see failure. I was surprised to learn that a lot of them expect some degree of failure and loss as part of their overall plan. I thought to myself, "who goes into any kind of venture thinking about failing?" That goes against everything we're taught as Americans, for crying out loud! In fact, as an attorney I've seen many small business owners liquidate their retirements, mortgage their underwear and practically sell their children to keep their businesses afloat, even when they KNOW that it's going to fold! Many times after the business closes, they still don't want to admit that they failed. Generally, wealthy people appear to be able to look at the failure for what it is, learn from it, change their behavior accordingly and start over.

Again, that goes against everything we have been taught. We Americans don't quit and we don't give up, right? I know that's true for me. I was always told to never give up, thank you Grandpa and Winston Churchill. As a result, I've banged my head against the wall, continuing to work at jobs that my gut was telling me to quit because I didn't want to leave my employer hanging. Generally, at the expense of my well-being. That's just what we are brought up learning, be on time, get an education, work hard, do the right thing, do not quit and you will eventually succeed. Sound familiar? Yes, I thought so.

Well, maybe that's what the 99% has been taught. The 1% know better. Now, I'm not saying they don't believe in working hard and the American dream. I'm saying they know that failure is inevitable at some point. Wealthy people understand the true nature of risk. They know that their identity is not tied to the success of any given venture and that sometimes you have to take a risk if you are going to succeed in a big way. If they start a business, invest in something or do a deal that starts to go bad, they generally have no problem changing gears and taking a different path, even if that means closing the business altogether. They do their best to "protect their downside" or hedge their bets and then, they go for it!

Again, a hard lesson, and one I've had to learn over and over again, was accepting failure. It took a long time for me to understand that when a plan fell through, it didn't mean I was less than, it just meant my plan didn't work! It seems like I've been learning this lesson since I graduated from high school. However, if you are asking yourself the right questions, sooner or later you'll figure it out. I did eventually learn that the 1% do not see failure as a permanent black mark on their identity. They see it as a learning experience that helps them adjust their course of action. What it boils down to is that generally, they aren't afraid to fail. So what's the message? Well, the 1% isn't afraid to fail, and you shouldn't be either.

The second aspect of failure that is important to remember is that as you fail and recover, you begin to see yourself as resilient. So, what exactly does that mean? The definition of resilient is *capable of withstanding shock without permanent deformation or rupture, tending to recover from, or adjust easily to,* misfortune *or change*. Resilience is key to survival in this world because, as we've discussed before, everyone fails and life can throw you some pretty serious curve balls. That means, if you can build up your resilience muscle, you are way, WAY ahead of the game! You build that muscle by falling down and getting back up, learning from your mistakes and then putting one foot in front of the other. It sounds hard, but it really is necessary that you learn this skill.

Trust me, I know what I'm talking about. In any given area of my life, I have failed spectacularly at one time or another. Oh boy, if I wrote about all my failures, you could run laps around the manuscript. I will admit that when I was in the thick of each one, there is no way you could've ever convinced me that I would be thankful for it one day. Not a chance! However, the truth is that none of those failures killed me and each of them taught me something valuable that helped me become the person I am today. In fact, the most valuable lesson I learned from each failure is first and foremost, I could survive failing! The world continued to turn and I continued to put one foot in front of the other. I just kept breathing and moving forward. Sooner or later, I recovered and the alternative was usually exactly what I needed.

What's the lesson we are trying to learn here? It's this: if you are going to fail, and you are, fail well, and the key to failing well is intention. That probably sounds like a stupid sentence, right? Truthfully, reading it makes me laugh. There's probably somebody out there saying "this woman is a bonehead, 'failing well' is an oxymoron, it doesn't make any sense." Well, maybe ... but, I do know that we are all going to fail, right? We've established that. So, if we are going to fail anyway, we might as well "protect our downside" and get as much out of our failures as possible. This is where intention comes into play. When your intention is right, in any situation, you really can't lose, even if you fail.

Alright, let's talk about intention. “Intent” is a term I really got to know in law school. I became aware of the value of intent when studying criminal law and this is the best way I can think of to explain it. Committing a “specific intent” crime meant you were intentionally trying to do something, usually something pretty bad, to another person. Let's take homicide, for example. If you commit a specific intent crime, the punishment is the worst you can get under the law. This includes the death penalty. On the other hand, if you commit a crime without the intent to do so, say involuntary manslaughter, you will still get punished but your punishment will be much less than in a specific intent crime. This demonstrates the value of intent. This property of intention is true in every area of your life, not just in the world of criminal law. It's the principle of right and wrong, that is intention. So, if you set your intention based on your values before you take action, you'll be all right no matter what!

At the end of the day remember, if you make a mistake or fall off of the budget wagon, don't beat yourself up. Just like dieting, creating a budget and committing to that lifestyle change of careful money management may not happen overnight. You will fall down and have to work at it but, eventually you will get the hang of it. If you still need something to inspire you, think of the great white shark. Of all the living things on earth, the great white shark is an amazing, powerful and resilient survivor. How does it survive? Resilience. It never stops moving forward. When you fall down and feel like not getting back up, remember the great white shark and keep moving forward!

Chapter 6 – A little help from the Flintstones

When I was a kid, my Mom would buy us those Flintstones chewable vitamins when we were looking pale or weird. Remember those? In my mind's eye, I can clearly see those little purple and pink Freds and Wilmas in the that little glass jar. They still make them today but, they just aren't the same. Thinking back, I don't really recall them tasting all that great but hey, it was Fred Flintstone! I was all about cartoons and I would've eaten a liver and Brussels sprout sandwich if it looked like Bugs Bunny.

So, what's the point? Well, this chapter is really about the basics of investing, which can be a little boring, that's true. A good way to spice up an otherwise dull topic is to think of investing in a more creative way, like financial vitamins and supplements. The vitamin and supplement analogy also goes along with the idea of weight loss and overall financial health. It works like this: when you finally have some disposable income, or breathing room in your Spanx, it's time to work on figuring out what to do with it.

Remember from Chapter 1, the rule is to not just save it, but to invest it. Investing boosts the value of your bank account like vitamins and supplements boost your overall health and weight loss. Get it? When you start to realize the huge difference investing can make in your financial bottom line, believe me, you'll get excited about it.

Let me start this chapter off by saying that I am not a financial planner, financial advisor or securities broker. I would never suggest that anyone go invest in the stock market on their own if they have no experience in picking stocks or investing. Having said that, I do know a few basics about investing that I feel I can pass onto you safely.

Now pay close attention. I'm about to teach you the vitamin principle, which is the most important concept in money management. It will significantly boost your investing, savings and retirement planning. Okay, it doesn't really have anything to do with vitamins but it is the engine you can use to make your money grow much, much faster. It's a concept called compound interest and it's very important that you understand it because it's how regular people turn themselves into millionaires and it can be a beautiful thing! The simplest definition is “an amount paid on the principal which is added to the principal and earns interest from that point forward.” Wonderful!!! For those of you who are entirely new to these concepts, your principal is the amount you start with. So, if you save $1,000 to open an IRA with, your principal is $1,000. If the account earns 6% in the first month, your account balance is now $1,060. Since the return (or dividend, the $60), of your IRA has to be reinvested, your IRA company will use that money to buy more shares and your principal is now increased. Get it?

Building on the idea of compound interest is the old adage, “remember that it’s not *timing* the market, it’s *time in* the market.” I’ve been investing money long enough to know that statement is true. Keeping your money invested allows the principle of compound interest to work. So, as soon as possible, create a budget and include an amount to save and/or invest, this is how you pay yourself first. Every month, you should be taking your savings and investing it. The earlier you start saving in this way, the more you can accumulate for retirement and the quicker you will begin to boost your bank account. Of course, there are lots of reasons to save and invest, but for our purposes, we are going to assume your goal is to save for retirement.

How do you get started? The best way is to start from where you are right now. If your employer has a 401(k), Roth 401(k) or deferred compensation plan like a 457(b) or 403(b) plan, you should be contributing to it and working toward making the maximum contribution possible. Investing in these plans is a wonderful option because you can have the contribution deducted directly from your payroll before it gets to you. This is like getting the benefit of a vitamin without actually having to take the pill, which can taste really bad. Someone is adding it in to your diet without you even realizing it. An added bonus is that these plans also come with tax benefits that can work out to a big tax savings for you. Typically, any funds you put in won't be taxed until you draw them out at retirement. Except the Roth 401(k). With that type of investment, you put money in after you pay taxes on it. Your employer can also contribute to your Roth 401(k), but those contributions are not tax free, it makes sense, if you think about it.

There is one big caveat that you should be aware of when investing in an employer sponsored plan. In fact, you should be concerned with this issue with any financial investment or financial advisor, manager, planner and broker: management fees. I think a lot of people don't realize that just because a 401(k) or deferred compensation plan is employer sponsored, it can still include some pretty hefty management fees. When you have money to invest, whether you have the option to invest in an employer based plan or your only option is an independent plan, you should be making sure that you understand what fees you will be paying before you invest. The fees could seem minimal but, make no mistake, they add up. If you know what percentage of fees you will be paying and you know how much you intend to invest, you can figure out how much the fees will wind up costing you, assuming an average rate of return of 6%. Management fees can eat up 50% to 70% of your returns over time. Beware of the seemingly "small" management fee. Avoid it as best you can.

Remember, your employer does not handle the management of the plan's assets, they simply sponsor it but they should have contact information for the plan administrator. Use it! Call and make sure they explain to you how much the management fees are, how are they calculated? What's the percentage and when are they assessed? Ask it this way, "how do I pay for my account to be administered?" Also, make sure you keep an eye on your statements and work to figure out what they mean. I will tell you, after years of looking at investment statements of all kinds, they are about as confusing as any legal document I've ever seen. It seems to me that they are designed to be more confusing than a tax return. Don't tell anyone in the financial industry I said that, but I swear it's true. If you can't understand your statement, call the plan administrator or the investment company and make them explain it to you. They are getting paid well and they work for you. Without your money, they would have no business so, they can take the time to explain your statement. This is true for employer sponsored plans and any company you invest with privately, too.

There are two very important reasons why I suggest investing with your employer, if possible. The first is because the contribution is generally taken out of your pay before you ever see it and that is a really big deal. Remember the nasty tasting vitamin. When you get the benefit of the vitamin without having to actually take the pill, winner winner, chicken dinner! If you get used to the contribution, you won't miss it. Second, absolutely DO NOT miss out on the employer contribution. Even if you can't contribute the allowed maximum amount, you should still contribute enough to get your full employer match (they are allowed to match up to 6%). That is FREE money; DO NOT leave it on the table unless the management fees would eat it up.

If you don't have the option of an employer sponsored investor plan, you can do it yourself. For people who have never invested before and have no desire to learn how to do it, I suggest heading over to Vanguard and opening up a Roth Individual Retirement Account. If you are looking at another company, make sure they offer *no load* investment options. Think back to Chapter 1, the load is the fee that is paid to the fund manager for the work they do managing the fund. Ideally, the fund manager will use his or her expertise to maximize the return on the fund. The truth is, there are very few managers who have ever beaten the market, which is why I would avoid specialized mutual funds. For those of us who are just getting started and not trained in the financial services industry, I would suggest sticking with no load mutual index funds.

Okay, so what is a mutual fund? It's a little technical but, a mutual fund is an account that people like you and me can invest in by paying money to the mutual fund and getting shares in return.

The number of shares we buy determines how much of the fund we own. Once our money is in the fund, it gets pooled together with all the money from everyone else who, like us, also purchased shares of the fund. Then the mutual fund manager invests all the money in the fund in stocks, bonds, etc. Our dividend, or payout, depends on how the fund performs. If it makes money, that profit is paid to everyone who owns shares in the fund based on how many shares they own. Full disclosure, the same is true if it loses money. Why does this benefit you? Because, you can take advantage of the fund's purchase of different securities, equities, etc., without having to spend time learning how to invest on your own and with a far cheaper buy in. The argument is that the fund has hired a manager who has a lot of experience managing money and is really good at it. That can be true but remember, very few managers have ever beaten the market over time.

Your next question might be, what is an index fund? A simple way for regular people, like you and me, to diversify their investments is by investing in index funds. These are funds that track a financial market, or index. For example, the most well known index I can think of is the S&P 500. Who hasn't been watching the news and heard that name? The S&P 500 is Standard & Poor's list of 500 companies with stocks that trade on the stock exchange, the New York Stock Exchange or the NASDAQ. It's been around since 1923 and the companies that are listed on it are selected by a committee based on certain criteria. They are generally blue chip stocks, meaning they are stocks issued by financially sound, well established companies.

Index funds hold their stocks in a mirror image of the index they are tracking. Based on the amount of money available in the fund, the fund manager will buy a percentage of individual stocks in the same proportion as the index they are tracking. Complicated, right? That's the great thing about an index fund; someone else figures all that stuff out for you, all you have to do is buy shares in the fund. This is called passive investing and some people in the financial industry are strongly against it. I think it's a great way for someone who is new to investing to break into the market in a safe, manageable way.

You can buy index funds through Vanguard and direct investing companies like Ameritrade but do your homework first. You may have to save up enough to buy into the fund since most companies require a minimum investment amount prior to offering a bigger selection of funds to invest in. You can always buy individual shares of blue chip stocks, but be very careful! I would never suggest investing in individual stocks unless you really know what you are doing. You can seriously lose your shirt and then you'll be shirtless! Nobody wants that! The idea is to start by buying shares of a fund that has a proven track record and a reasonable buy in amount. Vanguard offers a minimum buy in of $1,000 for their Target Retirement Funds. It doesn't get any cheaper than that! When your account grows over time, you can upgrade if you choose to. Just make sure you are aware of the tax consequences when you sell shares since you will be taxed on whatever income you earned over the life of the investment.

There is also another diversification option you can invest in called exchange traded funds (ETFs). They are relatively new to the world of the personal investor but this type of investment works like a mutual fund in that it can track an index, too. The main difference is that its shares are traded like stocks on the stock exchange. You can check with your investment company to see what ETFs they have available for purchase, if you like.

You don't have to start off buying individual stocks or index funds, you just need to start investing. Find out what you have to work with based on the amount of money you have and go from there. Most of the companies who are providing direct investment services (allowing people to invest on their own), have great customer service departments who can answer lots of questions for you. Don't be afraid to call them up and ask them any question you want. They are generally very helpful and again, they work for you.

So, you've got an idea of what type of investment to buy, now you need to pick the type of investment account you want to use. Of course, this assumes you can't or don't want to invest in your employer sponsored plan. The three main types of accounts are a regular brokerage or investment account, an IRA (individual retirement account), or a Roth IRA. For a chart showing the basic comparison of the three most popular types of investment accounts, see Figure 2. You can go to Vanguard and open any one of these accounts online and fund it with an online funds transfer from your bank. Before you do, though, you need to take a few things into consideration. First, you need to think about your tax situation. Keep that in mind while you look at the chart below.

Figure 2 - Investment Account Comparison Chart

Feature	Brokerage	IRA	Roth IRA	401(k)	Roth 401(k)
Contribution limit 49 years of age or less	None	$6,000.00	$6,000.00	$19,500.00	$19,500.00
Contribution limit 50 years of age or older	None	$7,000.00	$7,000.00	$26,000.00	$26,000.00
Contribution deadline	None	4/15 of next tax year	4/15 of next tax year	Deducted from payroll	Deducted from payroll
Tax deferral	No tax benefit	Yes, pre-tax dollars	No, post-tax dollars	Yes, pre-tax dollars	No, for employee contribution only
Taxable growth	Yes	Yes, but taxed on distribution	No!! Yay!! Never taxed!	Yes, but taxed on distribution	No, for employee contribution
Mandatory age for distribution	N/A	72 but you can start at 59.5	59 1/2 - NO required minimum distribution!	70.5 but you can begin at 59.5	Typically, the same as regular 401(k)
Penalty for early withdrawals	N/A	Yes (with some exceptions)	Yes, ***unless*** you only withdraw your contributions (with some exceptions)	Yes, but loans are possible in certain circumstances; watch out for taxes on loan!	Typically, the same as regular 401(k)

I've heard people say that it's not how much money you make that matters, it's how much you get to keep. Incidentally, I agree wholeheartedly with that statement. The lesson is that sooner or later, the tax man cometh. If you open a regular brokerage account and you make money off of your investments, and I hope you do, then you will pay taxes on those earnings. Remember, if you choose to open a regular brokerage account, use the dividend reinvestment plan (called a DRIP). This feature allows the company that holds your account to reinvest your earnings back into your account. This means that when your account pays a dividend you will "buy more shares," of mutual funds or ETFs. That's definitely the way to go unless you need the income right away—which you will be taxed on! The goal, however is to defer paying taxes on your investments until you are in the lowest possible tax bracket, right? If that's the case, you need to consider an IRA.

Okay, you probably already know that an IRA is an individual retirement account, right? What is the benefit of using an IRA as a savings vehicle? Well, simply put, tax deferment. Before I get into IRAs, I think it's important to tell you that there are a lot of seemingly complicated laws regarding IRAs, 401(k)s and other investment accounts. This guide is designed to be a basic guide. You should do your homework before you commit to one type of account. If you have a tax professional, it's a good idea to talk to them and get some advice about what type of account to use based on your annual income, since tax deductions phase out at certain income levels. If you don't have a tax professional, I would consider getting one as your assets begin to grow.

Having said that, if you make less than $100,000 a year, you are probably safe in using any retirement savings account. Remember, check with your employer and see if they have a plan you can contribute to, and contribute at least the minimum amount to get the employer match (as long as the management fees on the plan are not too high).

In my opinion, an IRA is a wonderful thing for those of us who make up the 99%. You don't have age limits for starting one and generally, the maximum contribution limit is the best most of us can do when we start out investing, anyway. My IRA of choice is by far, the Roth IRA. I've had one for years and if you are contemplating which type of IRA to open, I believe it's the best one hands down. It can also double as your emergency fund because it is the only type of investment account you can open that you can withdraw your ***contributions*** from without penalty at any time, and ***without paying tax on it!*** The catch is you have to keep track of your contributions to make sure you can prove that the money you withdraw is from your contributions, not earnings. If you are keeping the 5498 forms your IRA custodian sends you every year, you should be fine. I scan them and keep them on my hard drive for convenience.

Of course, withdrawing contributions from your Roth IRA should be a last resort, meaning a true emergency. I don't know about you but in my opinion, an emergency is not a brand new car or fancy vacation, or whatever. An emergency generally means a life and death situation, like if you need a kidney right away or something. If you lose your job and you get to the point where your unemployment benefits have run out and you have absolutely no choice but to dip into your emergency fund, well so be it. As long as you are following all of the other rules of this book, then I can forgive using some of your Roth IRA contribution funds to keep yourself afloat until you can get back to a positive cash flow situation. For anything else, look at the 4 Question Flow Chart at the end of this book.

Note that a 457 deferred compensation plan is like a 401(k) but for government employers. Also, a 403(b) plan is similar to a 457 or 401(k), it's just for public education employers. To learn more about the specific features of these plans, check with your plan administrator.

Again, don't forget the value of compound interest. Remember, this principle works for any type of account that pays you interest. The idea is to make it work for you through investing, too. You do this by investing in the right products, through carefully chosen accounts that re-invest your earnings (don't forget to turn on the DRIP option). Always remember this, compound interest works in the opposite direction, too. For example, when you crank up your credit card balances without paying them down and you pay interest every month, whatever you bought on the card begins to go up in price even after you've bought it. The price of that dinner out or that cute pair of boots that were on sale compounds every time you are charged interest. My rule of thumb is this:

"People should be paying you interest, not the other way around!"

A fitting way to end the chapter on investing!

Chapter 7 – Your credit and you: credit 101

Well, we have arrived at the last frontier of personal finance, your credit. If I had a nickel for every time I've had someone say to me, "how will this affect my credit?", I would be the richest person in the universe! Okay, maybe not but, you get the point. Ah, credit, that mysterious, effervescent thing that lives in an impenetrable world also known as Equifax, Transunion and Experian. Hopefully, this chapter will de-mystify credit a little and help you figure out how to get, and keep, your credit in top shape.

It might help us to think about credit for just a moment. What constitutes credit? The dictionary defines it as "the ability of a customer to obtain goods or services before payment, based on the trust that payment will be made in the future." By this definition, a creditor is any company, person, or entity who provides something you'll have to pay for after you actually have the item or service in hand. Creditors can be private individuals, utility companies, stores, doctors, hospitals, schools and the government (yay, taxes!!), or any taxing agency. Though it may seem like I am anti-credit, the truth is that credit is not always a bad thing. It can help you get something big that you need but would take you years and years to save for, like a college education or a house. However, credit and debt go hand in hand and for me, debt is pretty much a four-letter word. But, I digress …

Before I get started talking about credit, full disclosure, you should know that the only reason I keep a good eye on my credit is solely for security reasons. I really don't worry about my credit. I don't need to. I live by my philosophy and principles of money management which means I really don't have a lot of debt and rarely take on new debt. When I do, I work diligently to pay it off. Generally, I try to avoid debt completely. So, when you don't need to borrow money, you don't need to worry about your credit. Of course, there are exceptions to that rule. For example, you may need good credit to get a job, especially one with a security clearance or in the financial industry. Obviously, your credit will determine your interest rates for mortgages and car loans and how much it will cost you to borrow money. Your credit score can also affect your insurance rates, too. No matter what, you should at least keep an eye on your credit. But, for those who still depend on credit as a part of their financial plan, read on!

When we talk about our credit, we're really talking about two components that make up credit, as we understand it. Your credit report and your credit score. It's important to know that these are two entirely different things but, your credit score does not exist without your credit report. Your credit score is calculated from the information in your credit report. So, that's where we need to start, with your credit report.

The history of credit reports

Just because I'm kind of a nerd this way, I wanted to give you a brief history of credit reports in America. I find this kind of stuff interesting and hopefully, you will, too! Okay, well ... just humor me for a minute.

Of course, there have been credit reports since there's been credit, and there's been credit since cavemen have been buying, selling and trading loincloths, or saber toothed tiger repellent, or whatever. However, credit reports as we know them in this modern age, evolved after World War II. A guy named Mark Furletti did a great paper on the history of credit reporting back in 2002 that pretty much covers it. Again, I find this stuff interesting but, I'll give you the short version based on Furletti's paper, just in case you are already starting to doze.

Beginning in the 1950s different industries got together locally and created "co-ops" for the purpose of collecting information on consumers. Incidentally, these co-ops later became known as credit bureaus. They are also known as consumer reporting agencies (as in the Fair Credit Reporting Act), and the more common credit reporting agency (CRA). These are all names for the same thing, just so we're clear.

Credit reports started with paper files. These co-ops would employ people to collect all kinds of information about customers like weddings, births, marriages, promotions, arrests, etc. The co-ops would often have newspaper clippings with information about customers in their files. Typically, they were industry specific and did not share their files with other industries, competitors, etc. Their main goal was to collect personal information about consumers that the creditor would use to determine whether or not they were sound credit risks. As you can imagine, the credit bureaus and their data collection practices could be a little unethical at times, ahem.

By the end of the 1960s, credit agencies were so numerous, and their data collection practices had become so questionable, that Congress responded by passing the Fair Credit Reporting Act in 1970.[7] The FCRA was the first shot at regulating CRAs which, prior to 1970 had been unregulated. Whether or not the regulations were successfully enforced, that's another thing altogether.

During the 1980s, credit bureaus began to get more efficient with the advent of computers and technology. Eventually, the bigger regional bureaus began to gobble up the small bureaus until the three main agencies emerged as the nationwide CRAs we have today. There are still many different local, regional or industry specific CRAs. However, the majority of the credit agency market is dominated by the three national CRAs: Transunion, Equifax and Experian, (which used to be TRW, remember them?). As night follows day, these agencies began to expand their business and revenue by selling information across industries.[8]

CRA basics

So, your credit report has evolved from a paper file with

---

[7] 15 U.S.C. §1681

[8] Furletti, Mark J. "An Overview and History of Credit Reporting." *SSRN Electronic Journal SSRN Journal* (2002): 1-16. Web.

subjective information thrown into it by shady characters to a digital report with accumulated information that is now regulated, standardized and generally easier to manage. Thanks to the Fair Credit Reporting Act of 1970, this is the information you can generally expect to find in your credit report that should be reported consistently:

— Creditor name, address and account number (full or partial).

— Type of credit account (revolving/credit card, mortgage, auto loan, etc.).

— Date the account was opened, status of the account.

— Payment history, payment amount, terms.

— Joint or individual, high balance amount, original balance.

Remember, the CRAs, are NOT government agencies. They are private agencies that are regulated by the government. That means that as long as the credit reports they generate are following the laws, the credit reports can be structured and formatted anyway the agency sees fit. Each of the three national agencies are competing with each other so they try to maximize whatever they are featuring on their reports. This means they use different, proprietary lingo, too. This, in my opinion, can be a pain but, once you get used to it you can navigate the reports with relative ease.

Again, the information you can find on your credit report should ideally be consistent throughout CRAs. Unfortunately, there is no guarantee that every CRA will include all debts on your report. Remember that CRAs are businesses who CHARGE for their services. So, say a creditor wants immediate access to a particular agency's credit reports, they have to pay for that service. They also have to pay to report, too. Remember that creditors generally only report once every 30 days so a good rule of thumb is that a debt generally isn't reported as delinquent until it is 30 days past due. This also means that if you need to work on your credit before a major purchase, you should begin at least six months beforehand.

There is no law that says a creditor has to report to a CRA or that all agencies must report all accounts that creditors report to any one credit agency. Now that we know that the information on your credit report depends on the creditors who report it and that creditors do not have to report to all three national CRAs, we have an idea of how to start managing our credit. The key to this is to make sure you are checking with each of the three national credit reporting agencies every four months.

It is important to understand that the CRA and the creditor control your credit report. This means that only the CRA and/or the creditor themselves can change, remove or update information on your credit report. A creditor can be the original creditor, say the doctor who removed your brother-in-law's tattoo of his first wife's name, or the next creditor who buys the debt from Dr. Ink. We'll call that creditor DBDCA (short for Dirt Bag Debt Collectors of America, Inc.). Now, DBDCA bought the old debt from Dr. Ink for $0.15 on the dollar. DBDCA turns around and starts hassling brother-in-law for payment of the FULL AMOUNT of the original debt, plus whatever fees they feel the need to tack on. DBDCA is now the creditor on that debt and can report it to any CRA any time they want. DBDCA, and companies like them, make big bucks buying old debt and collecting on it.

The last thing for you to be aware of regarding credit reporting agencies is that any creditor can use any credit reporting agency. This means that some creditors, for example industry specific creditors, may not use a national credit reporting agency. However, if a creditor, employer or etc., makes a negative determination about your application based on any credit report from any CRA, they have to tell you about it. Then, by law you can request a copy of the credit report that the creditor relied on to make the decision. Generally, one of the three national CRAs are checked when you've applied for a job, loan or whatever.

How do I start?

Like the chapter on investing, this chapter is intended to be a basic guide to managing and repairing your credit. You should understand that there is a lot more information out there that may be helpful to you depending on your situation. You should also understand that there might be laws in your state that could benefit you when managing your creditors, as well. It might not be a bad idea for you to hop on the Internet and see what might be available at the state level, too. You might be surprised at the resources your state has to offer for consumers. Having said that, we can start with the basics.

Step #1

First and foremost, understand that really no one can do more to repair your credit than you. The truth is that as an attorney, I can't do much more to repair your credit than you can, short of threatening to sue, or actually suing the creditor or CRA (which would cost you a small fortune in legal fees and may not be the correct remedy anyway). People ask me about credit repair all the time and I tell them the same thing, you need to work on this yourself, don't spend money hiring someone to do something you can do for free. There are laws in place that are designed to make sure your credit report is accurate. All you need is a little education on how the laws work and you can do as much as anyone to repair your credit. It's also true that the best person to monitor your credit is you. I wouldn't pay anyone to do that for me, either.

Now is a good time to talk about credit repair scams. If someone, or some company, tells you that they can remove legitimate negative entries from your credit report, they are violating multiple federal laws! There are so many scammers out there who say they can do things that they really can't under the law. Be very wary of hiring anyone that makes this claim. A lot of times they'll say, "we've found a loophole that we can use to get rid of bad credit mistakes." If someone says that to you, run! If you don't, you could find yourself in some trouble and out a lot of cash. Most of the time if something sounds too good to be true, it usually is. If you are trying to change your credit by manipulating your credit report in a dishonest way, you could be committing fraud. Just don't do it.

Now, there is a fine distinction that you should understand because the scammers definitely use this to their advantage. Here it is: a legitimate negative entry on your credit report **cannot** be removed. You just have to wait it out. A negative entry that is the result of a mistake or a debt that cannot be validated **can** be removed.

Does that make sense? Do you see how a scammer could make it seem like they could do something they can't, then soak you for a bunch of money and leave you with the original debt AND out the money you paid them to fix it. Get it? If not, hopefully it will become a little less murky a little later in the chapter.

Finally, there are specific laws in place that require "debt settlement agencies" and/or "credit repair agencies" to disclose fee schedules and the specific services they provide to their customers. They have to tell their customers how much time it will take to complete their services, too. See the Credit Repair Organization Act 15 U.S.C. 1679. Familiarize yourself with that law before you hire any third party to help you repair your credit. We'll talk more about this in the section of this book titled "Credit Counseling

Agencies."

Step #2

I call this one "The Four Month Rule." Thanks to the Fair and Accurate Credit Transaction Act of 2003 (FACT Act), each of the three national CRAs are required by law to give you a copy of your credit report every year, for free! You can get it online at www.annualcreditreport.com. Make sure you are using the correct website. There are a lot of scam websites out there so make sure you are using the right one. You should never be asked for a credit card when running your free credit report. You should be getting a credit report from each of the three CRAs every four months. Put it on your calendar like this:

January — Equifax

May — Experian

September — Transunion

Following this schedule allows you to monitor your credit report yourself. For free. You should be monitoring it for two things, security and accuracy. First, be on the look-out for identity theft. If you are keeping an eye on your credit report, you will catch that kind of activity sooner rather than later. Second, you should be checking it to make sure the information that's reported on it is right.

Remember to check the accuracy of ALL the information on the report. This means you should make sure your name, address, date of birth and employment information are all correct and spelled exactly the same on all reports. A study conducted by the Federal Trade Commission in 2013 indicated that 1 in 5 consumers had an error on at least one of their credit reports. Additionally, 5% of consumers had errors on their credit reports that would result in higher interest rates for loans, insurance, etc.[9] A slight spelling error could result in a huge problem if it meant that someone else's debts are reported on your credit report. Always check and make sure that your basic information is reported correctly. If you find a mistake, dispute it immediately. Remember, that holy grail of entries on a credit report is "paid as agreed," this is the ideal account status and what you should be shooting for.

Step #3

You've found an error or a negative entry, what now? Well,

---

[9] "FTC Study," Federal Trade Commission, accessed October 12, 2015, https://www.ftc.gov/news-events/press-releases/2013/02/ftc-study-five-percent-consumers-had-errors-their-credit-reports.

this is where things get a little more tricky. Remember when we talked about the difference between a legitimate negative entry and an error? The first thing you have to understand is that legitimate negative entries are on your credit report for the length of time required by law. By legitimate, I mean that you owe the debt, whatever negative treatment of the debt that's on your report is accurate (so, it's reported as 30 days late and you were 30 days late paying it), and the debt can be validated and/or verified.

If the negative entry is legitimate, it will be on your credit for a set length of time. Here are the timelines for reporting negative entries according to the FCRA:

— 7 years for adverse information, accounts placed for collection or charged off, civil lawsuits/judgments (this includes defaults on court ordered child support), records for arrest and paid tax liens.

— 10 years for Bankruptcies!

Hard credit inquiries will stay on your credit for 2 years. Hard inquiries happen when a creditor or lender officially checks your credit. Be careful with allowing creditors to do hard credit inquiries. They will stay on your credit and can bring down your credit score so avoid them unless it's absolutely necessary.

Understand that the clock resets on the negative entry <u>every time</u> it's reported. So, if you are late paying Dr. Ink in January and he reports it as late, then you are late again in February, which he also reports, the 7-year clock runs from the most recent late payment in February. The clock starts on each individual account from the date of the last reported activity, too. This is true even if there is more than one creditor for a single account. For example, if Dr. Ink sold the debt to DBDCA in March, they can start reporting the missed payments, too. You will have the negative entry on your report from Dr. Ink in starting February and DBDCA starting in March. The main thing to remember is <u>if the negative entry is legitimate and can be validated, you just have to wait it out.</u>

If you have determined that the negative entry is not legitimate, you can dispute it. How do you determite if the entry is not legitimate? Start by asking if you really owe the debt. If it looks like it is someone else's debt or its older than 7 years, dispute it immediately. If it could be a debt that you think you might owe but you aren't sure, try to identify it. That's usually not too difficult if the entry is by the original creditor. If it's been sold to a debt collector, it could be tricky. A debt collector will often assign a new in-house account number to debts they purchase and/or leave out information about it like when it originated and what it was for, and so on. This makes it harder to identify the debt and the original creditor. If you recognize the debt, determine if you have a reason to dispute it. For example, you actually did pay Dr. Ink on time and your check was cashed but payment was keyed to the wrong account. That is grounds for dispute with the original creditor.

Now, if it has been sold to a debt collector they are required by law to validate the debt. The Fair Debt Collection Practices Act states that if a consumer disputes a debt, the debt collector must respond with verification of the debt within 30 days. They have to "obtain verification of the debt" and mail a copy of it to the consumer, that's you, by the way! (See FDCPA 15 U.S.C. §1692g) The bonus is that the debt collector has to stop all debt collection efforts until the debt is validated. We can assume that the original creditor should be able to easily verify the debt. However, this is not always true for debt collectors who buy debt in bulk, often for pennies on the dollar. They aren't always careful about making sure they have the paperwork to validate the debts they buy. If they can't validate it, time to dispute it!

Please note that just because an original creditor (like Dr. Ink), has charged off or sold a debt to a debt collector (like DBDCA), that doesn't mean that you no longer owe the debt. Likewise, just because a debt collector can't validate a debt doesn't mean that you no longer owe the debt. That has to do with the statute of limitations that applies to your debt or, whether or not the debt is time barred. My goal with this chapter is to explain the ins and outs of credit reports, not the statute of limitations on debts. For more information on whether or not you owe the debt, check with a local bankruptcy attorney.

Step #4

How do you go about disputing a debt or negative entry? Well, to start with, always dispute it with the CRA <u>and</u> the creditor (this includes the original creditor or anyone who bought the debt from the original creditor). Make sure you are disputing the negative entry with the correct CRA. Do not dispute an error with a CRA that does not have the error on the credit report they generated. That could do more harm than good. It would be a good idea to check that CRA's dispute policy as well. They may ask you to send in a utility bill or something to prove your identity. Don't send your full social security number but, try to comply with their policy to expedite the dispute process. Just be smart about what you send in. Also, it would be wise to take note that frivolous disputes with CRAs are not looked on favorably. You should only dispute a negative entry with a CRA if you know, or have good reason to believe, it is an erroneous entry, or if you know that the debt collector can't validate the debt. Once you dispute it with the CRA, they have to investigate it by law. The CRA also has to notify the creditor of the dispute within five days. Once the CRA notifies the creditor of the dispute, the creditor has to investigate it, too. After their investigation, they have to report back to the CRA and if the disputed debt is removed, the reporting CRA has to notify the nationwide CRAs of the removal of the entry. Now, why dispute it with the CRA and the creditor since the CRA has to notify the creditor anyway? Well, that way the dispute should become part of your record with the creditor and anyone who investigates the debt in the future should see your dispute in their records. Debt collectors must also provide a copy of the dispute to any CRA that is investigating the debt in the future.[10]

You can dispute the entry online, by telephone or in writing. I suggest always, ALWAYS doing it in writing—in fact send everything certified mail, return receipt requested. That's the smartest way to go. For a sample dispute letter from the Federal Trade Commission website, see Appendix B. Once you have sent in your notice of dispute, the CRA generally has 30 days to investigate it. Remember, any time you are dealing with your debts, creditors, CRAs or anything else having to do with your credit, DOCUMENT, DOCUMENT, DOCUMENT. It's a good rule of thumb to keep records on every debt. Always include copies of all documentation you've received (including proof of the debt), correspondence you've sent and thorough records about who you've talked to about the debt. Make sure you have the name, contact information, date, time and the basic gist written down for every conversation you have about your credit and/or debts. Also, it's a good idea to follow up on conversations in writing to make sure you're all on the same page (keep all your e-mails, too!).

Another important note about disputing entries on your credit report, never send your original documentation to anyone. Always

---

[10] FDCPA 15 U.S.C. §1692g

keep the originals and send copies. Something else to keep in mind is the contents of the dispute. We've already established that the investigating CRA can disregard the dispute if it is frivolous. It's good to note that they can consider a dispute frivolous if it doesn't have enough evidence to show why you are disputing the debt. Make sure you write a thorough explanation of your dispute. Attach documentation (not originals!), and make sure you ask for the results you want. Do you want the information corrected or do you want the debt removed entirely?

If you've done any research about the OSCAR system, you may be wondering if there are any tips or tricks you could use to "beat the system" somehow. I've seen a lot of information on the internet about how to structure your dispute documents to get around that system. OSCAR is a coding system designed to help deal with the volume of disputes that the CRAs have to manage. It works by assigning short codes to the dispute so the creditors and CRAs can communicate faster during the investigation process. It is definitely flawed, that's for sure! The good news is the Consumer Financial Protection Bureau is working on the investigation process to ensure accuracy. The best way to beat OSCAR is first, ask the creditor to validate or verify the debt. If they can't, try to get that information in writing and include it with your dispute letter to the CRA. The gold standard would be a copy of the contract, agreement or paperwork with your handwritten signature showing you owe the debt. Second, make sure your dispute letter is as thorough as possible. Don't rely on anyone, creditor or CRA, to do your thinking or advocating for you!

If, after the 30 days, the CRA determines through their investigation that your dispute is valid, they must remove the entry from your credit report. Huzzah! The CRA has to notify you of the results of the investigation in writing and send you another credit report reflecting the change in the disputed debt entry. If they find it is invalid, ask the CRA to provide a copy of the procedure they followed when investigating the dispute and a copy of the validation documentation they received from the creditor during the investigation. They are required to provide that according to the Fair Credit Reporting Act.

If the CRA doesn't rule in your favor, you always have the statement option. By law, you can have a statement of explanation or dispute placed in your credit report by way of explanation of the debt. Again, this is if the investigation doesn't resolve it. Note: it's important not to leave the statement in your credit report indefinitely, though. After a few years of good credit management, your negative entry will carry less weight so it's smart to remove the statement of explanation, rather than highlight your past history of bad credit. Just remember to put the statement on ALL three credit reports and don't forget to remove it from them all, too.

Debt collectors

If you find yourself in the unfortunate situation of having to deal with debt collectors, this part of the chapter is for you! There are very specific rules about what debt collectors can and cannot do when collecting a debt. This is also a good time for you to check and see if your state has specific laws about debt collectors. We are going to work with the federal law, the Fair Debt Collection Practices Act[11], for our purpose. The FDCPA applies to anyone who is in the business of debt collection but, it exempts any creditor collecting on their own debts. So, the FDCPA would not apply to Dr. Ink when he is collecting on his own debt, for example.

I've had clients tell me all sorts of stories about things debt

[11] 15 U.S.C. §1692

collectors have done to try to collect a debt. Typically, unethical debt collectors use emotional manipulation, fear or harassment to try to collect a debt. Some of the stories I've heard are truly unbelievable. The stories I've heard range from debt collectors calling at all hours, calling friends and family, and even posing as sheriff's deputies who are threatening to come and take them to jail. Lately, I've had several clients call and tell me that debt collectors have called them and told them a lawsuit has been filed against them and they need to appear in court (usually in another state). If they don't, when the judgment is entered against them, a warrant for their arrest will be issued. Pay close attention to the next statement because it's really important... YOU CAN'T GO TO JAIL FOR SIMPLY OWING MONEY. If someone is threatening you with an arrest warrant because you owe money, they are violating the FDCPA. They threaten, manipulate and harass because they CAN'T send you to jail. Think about it. If they could send you to jail, they would. So, if a debt collector tries to threaten you, hang up on them and screen your calls!

These are the things a debt collector <u>cannot</u> do, when collecting a debt according to the FDCPA:

1. Debt collectors can only contact you when it is not inconvenient. The presumption is not before 8:00 a.m. or after 9:00 p.m.
2. If you have an attorney, they have to contact your attorney.
3. They can't call you at work if you, or your boss (hopefully, it doesn't get that far!), tells them not to.
4. They can't contact third parties (except CRAs, etc.), this means your friends or family, unless they are co-signers of the debt.
5. If you tell them not to contact you they have to stop contacting you unless they are contacting you to tell you:
    a. That they are stopping efforts to collect the debt.
    b. To tell you they can still pursue normal remedies (they are **<u>about</u>** to sue you!!).
    c. To tell you they intend to pursue normal remedies (they **<u>are</u>** suing you!!).
6. They can't harass or abuse you. This means they can't:
    a. Use or threaten to use violence, or other criminal means to harm the physical person, reputation, or property of any person.

b. Use obscene or profane language or language the natural consequence of which is to abuse the hearer or reader.
c. Publish a list of consumers who allegedly refuse to pay debts, except to a consumer reporting agency.
d. Advertise for sale any debt to coerce payment of the debt.
e. Cause a telephone to ring or engage any person in telephone conversation repeatedly or continuously with intent to annoy, abuse, or harass any person at the called number.
f. Generally, make telephone calls without meaningful disclosure of the caller's identity.

7. They can't use any false, deceptive, or misleading representation or means in connection with the collection of any debt.
8. They generally may not use unfair or unconscionable means to collect or attempt to collect any debt.

If a debt collector does anything they shouldn't be doing, it's up to you to enforce the law. In order to do that, you need to document, document, document! Then contact the Federal Trade Commission or your state attorney general, and complain. You could also sue but, you will likely need to hire an attorney for that. However, if the actions of the debt collector are bad enough, then by all means, sue!

In many cases, the worst part of debt collection is mistaken information. Debt collectors buy debt in bulk, often without the necessary underlying paperwork. They buy it this way because it's cheaper for them and they can make more money from collections. This means they are not too concerned about the accuracy of their collections process. They are mostly concerned with getting paid and making money, right? It's your responsibility to make sure you are holding them accountable.

Now, debt collectors can contact you for the purpose of collecting a debt. When they do, make sure you get their contact info immediately. Get their name, telephone number and mailing address. Next, in order to begin holding them accountable, ask them to verify the debt in writing. Ask them on the phone and then again in writing (I would follow up in writing since they might not, uh, recall that you asked on the phone, capiche?). By law, THEY

MUST VERIFY THE DEBT WITHIN five (5) days from the date of the initial contact. Verification has to be in writing and must include:

1. The amount of the debt.
2. The name of the creditor.
3. A statement that you have 30 days to dispute it or it's considered a valid debt.
4. A statement that if the consumer notifies the creditor in writing within 30 days that any part of the debt is disputed the creditor will:
    a. Obtain verification and/or a copy of the judgment and mail it to the consumer.
    b. Will notify the consumer of the name of the original creditor if different from the current creditor.

Again, if you dispute the debt, all collection activities on the debt must stop until the debt collector has sent verification of the debt to the consumer (you!). They must also provide a copy of the dispute to any CRA that is investigating the debt in the future. Remember, this is why you dispute a debt with the CRA AND the debt collector!

It can be hard to enforce the rules under the FDCPA. If you

have questions about it, find a qualified attorney in your jurisdiction who can answer whatever questions you have about your situation and tell you whether or not you are entitled to any damages under the FDCPA. An attorney can also tell you if the laws in your state would be more helpful than the federal FDCPA. Also, you can contact your state attorney general, the Federal Trade Commission, and the Consumer Financial Protection Bureau. They might have resources you can use to help you resolve your situation. They may not file suit on your behalf but, they might have information that is vital to your situation.

So, just to recap, you should be checking your credit reports to make sure no debt collector is pursuing you in error. It's always good to have proof of your own debts and never, NEVER send your originals to anyone. Once it's gone, it's gone! Finally, a debt collector can be a legitimate creditor, if they actually have proof of the debt and keep good records (that means no robo-signed documents!). If that is the case, you may want to consider negotiating with the debt collector in order to stop the negative entries on your credit report. If you choose to do this, don't pay the debt until they provide the terms of repayment in writing. Make sure that the terms of repayment include removal of negative entries or as close to a "paid as agreed" notation as you can get. Finally, ALWAYS GET IT IN WRITING!

A word about old debt

Remember, just because a debt is older than seven years, that doesn't mean it can't sneak back up on you. There are all kinds of scenarios where a debt is still viable. Remember from earlier in the chapter that determining whether you still owe the debt depends on whether the statute of limitations has run. You may be asking, what is the statute of limitations? Well, that's state specific and you probably need to talk to a lawyer to figure that one out. Just be careful about getting into conversations with debt collectors on debts that are older than 5 years or you could become a victim of zombie debt. That is debt that was time barred but a crafty debt collector has figured out a way to revive. Again, talk to an attorney if you have questions about zombie debt in your state. Also, if the creditor has sued on the debt, the judgment may be hanging out there without your knowledge. Again, this is why it's important to be checking your credit report. If a judgment is out there, it will likely show up on your credit report. You should check with an attorney to find out if the judgment is still good.

Debt collectors are crafty. They will find ways to get around statute of limitations issues, paperwork issues, etc. If you live in a state where they can garnish your wages, they will try to figure out a way to try to do that, even if the debt is a mistake. Their interest is getting paid, regardless of whether or not their records are accurate. The best way to beat them is to avoid being in debt, if possible. In the meantime, it's important to keep an eye on your credit report to address any mistakes or errors as soon as possible because again, their interest is getting paid, not being accurate! An old debt can also be disputed for removal on your credit report so be on the look-out for them. However, understand the distinction that only time barred debts are a defense to lawsuits and that involves knowing the statute of limitations that applies to your debts. To learn more about that, talk to a local attorney.

My final word on debt collection is about medical debt. There are new rules for the reporting of medical debts that have just been announced by the Consumer Financial Protection Bureau. These rules will allow for a 180-day waiting period before a negative entry from a medical provider to any CRA is entered on your credit report. This is to allow time for the claim to be processed and paid by the debtor's insurance company. Also, medical debt can be viewed a little differently by creditors since medical debt is generally not something people get into intentionally. Most medical debt is unforeseen, unintentional and unwanted! This might be a good time to use the statement option on your credit reports (remember to include it in all three national CRAs). If you have a child with special needs, or you were in a car accident, for example, you might want to consider letting creditors know that is the reason for the past due medical debts. Be careful with this though, you might not want to let creditors know that your health might keep you from working, making you a poor credit risk.

Credit score

Usually, the one thing most people want to know is their credit score. I think it's widely believed that your "credit score" is standardized in some way, when it really isn't. In my opinion, "the credit score" is generally misunderstood. There can be as many different versions of your credit score as there are CRAs. Probably the main provider of credit scores, that most people have heard of, is FICO. That stands for Fair, Isaac and Company, and they began doling out credit scores in the 1980s. There are other companies that are springing up like VantageScore but for most people, FICO is the company that is the best known.

Unlike a credit report, you are not entitled to a free credit score. That's why you always have to pay for it. Credit scores are calculated using the information in your credit report that is plugged in to a proprietary formula to determine what type of credit risk you are, based on the other variables in the equation. This is why if you have no credit history, you typically have no credit score. The formulas and equations that each credit scoring company uses are different and can change, based on the purpose of the score. Different scoring systems can be created for different industries. For example, if you are opening a credit card, the type of credit score the creditor uses can be drastically different than an insurance company who is trying to determine your premiums. Make sense?

For our purposes, I think we can safely stick with FICO. Conveniently, FICO created a pie chart that shows what generally goes into figuring your credit score. I've included it here as Figure 3. Again, FICO is a company that sells credit scores so in order to figure out your credit score, you will need to order it from a company that provides it. Be careful with randomly ordering your score, though. First of all, it will cost you money. Second, you need to be careful with credit inquiries. When you are checking your credit score just for the sake of knowing it, make sure that checking your score will not result in a "hard inquiry" on your credit report. If it does, that can lower you score and will typically stay on your credit report for two years. It makes sense then, to avoid having too many credit inquiries in a short period of time.

Figure 3 - FICO Credit Score Components

Typically, a credit score ranges from 300 to 850, with a great credit score starting at 750 and above. As you can see from the chart, lots of things figure into your credit score but the biggest is your payment history! That means whether or not you pay your debts on time. Remember, nothing is better for your credit score than "paid as agreed" as the status of the account. The second most important aspect is the amounts owed or your debt to credit ratio. This is where things get complicated. When calculating your credit score, FICO is looking for proof that you are a good credit risk so they look at the following aspects, how many accounts you have open, the type of accounts, (mortgages, car loans, credit cards or medical debts), how old each account is and high balances on credit cards in relation to the amount of available credit. A large number of accounts with balances and recent high balances on credit cards can show that you are over extended and that is not a good thing. On the other hand, installment accounts, like mortgages and car loans, that show you had a high balance with a sustained period of on-time payments is a good thing.

You also need to think about your credit utilization ratio. This means, how much available credit you have in relation to the balances on those credit accounts. This means that if you have 2 credit cards that have $10,000 available limits and you only have $2,000 balances on each card, your balance owed is $4,000 and your credit utilization ratio is 20%. If you close one of the cards and maintain the $4,000 balance on the other, your credit utilization ratio is now 40%, you see? The higher your credit utilization ratio, the worse credit risk you are. However, no credit utilization ratio is a bad thing, too. That means you have no credit history. The rule of thumb I see frequently is that its best to keep your credit utilization ratio around 30%. I certainly wouldn't go too much higher than that.

Remember, if you pay off a credit card balance, it will generally take 30 days for it to show a zero balance on your credit report. It's also important to remember that the age of credit accounts are a factor in determining your credit score so opening a new credit card to increase your credit utilization ratio might not be a good thing. Should you keep some credit cards open but with low or no balances to increase your score? Maybe. You may want to consider whether or not you have too much available credit, as well. Will creditors look at your debt to income ratio when considering whether or not to give you a loan? Yes, absolutely. All this really just boils down to one thing, be smart about getting and using credit; and remember, the most important thing is to make sure you are paying your bills on time, or a day ahead of time, if possible!

This chart is just a basic list of the components of your FICO score. It does not take into consideration how many inquiries you've had recently or even the age of whatever negative entries you might have on your credit. Again, a credit score is a fluid thing. It can change very easily, at the drop of a hat really.

If you're getting ready to make a big purchase and you're trying for a low interest rate, that's when it's time to check your score. Here's what you should do. Go to your lender and ask them what credit scoring system they use. Ask them if they can help you get a soft inquiry credit score so you can get an estimate of where you are at. Again, make sure it's a soft inquiry so it will not affect your score. Remember to do this at least six months ahead of the time you estimate you will be buying the house, car or whatever. When you get your credit score, you start figuring out what you can do to beef it up. You can also Google "credit scoring" to learn more about how your score is calculated. So, all those instant access services that you hear about in all those TV commercials that are supposed to give you an instant credit score, you know the ones, right? Just remember, they don't take into account the fact that different creditors use different credit scoring methods to decide whether or not to loan you money or how much interest to charge. So, buyer beware! Buying services like that are almost never a good idea.

The most important thing to know about your credit score is the best way to improve it, right? Well, you do that by managing your finances carefully, living below your means and monitoring your credit regularly. Trying to beat the system is a whole lot harder than avoiding the issue in the first place.

Credit counseling agencies

This brings me to credit counseling agencies and the services they can provide. Since 2005, people who are filing for bankruptcy have to complete a credit counseling class before they can file. Because of that law, there are actually legitimate credit counseling agencies out there who really can help you develop a budget and figure out your basic financial situation.

However, the credit counseling industry is also full of scammers trying to relieve you of your hard earned cash. I've heard them called debt settlement companies, debt management agencies, or debt relief companies. Whatever you call them, they are the worst kind of predators. Just like debt collectors, they should know you are having financial problems (for crying out loud, you can't pay your bills! Duh!). To make things even worse, they go out and look for people who are in financial trouble AND THEN CHARGE THEM MORE MONEY to "help" negotiate debts on their behalf. I've had quite a few clients who paid thousands of dollars to debt settlement agencies just to wind up filing for bankruptcy anyway. I can't say it enough, beware the scammer!!

This practice is so unethical that the Federal Trade Commission has specific rules governing credit counseling agencies to keep the scamming to a minimum. Here are some of the things they are prohibited from doing. They can't charge you ahead of time for negotiating debts on your behalf. They can't make false promises. This means they can't tell you they can manage or negotiate all your debt, because they might not be able to (the creditor doesn't have to accept any negotiation of any debt). They can't pay themselves until they've at least created a debt management plan for you and/or negotiated a debt on your behalf, or made a payment to a creditor based on your debt management plan. They have to disclose their payment plan and fee schedule to you. They also have to tell you what their services include and how long it will take for you to see results. These rules now apply whether they called you or you called them. For more information, check out the Credit Repair Organization Act, or head to the FTC website and look for Telemarketing Sales Rules from 2010.[12]

---

[12] https://www.ftc.gov/tips-advice/business-center/guidance/debt-relief-services-telemarketing-sales-rule-guide-business.

My suggestion is to avoid this kind of debt management plan or service altogether. If you want a counselor to help you, head to the National Foundation for Credit Counseling website, www.nfcc.org, and find an accredited credit counseling agency who can really give you the help you need. Again, so-called "debt management" companies can't, and in most cases won't, do more for you than you can do for yourself. They don't have any more legal weight in negotiating or settling your debts than you do. Save yourself some grief, and cash, and handle it yourself or get advice from an accredited agency. Trust me, you really are your own best advocate and you are more capable than you think you are!

Identity theft

I feel like no chapter about credit management would be complete without some information about identity theft. I was a prosecutor for four years and I did criminal defense for seven. Add that to my bankruptcy experience and I am pretty familiar with identity theft and how it can happen. In my experience, identity theft usually happens in one of three ways. First, someone can swipe your information in an information breach. Nasty and irritating, but usually you can contain it if you've been monitoring your credit as I suggested earlier in this chapter.

Second, you could lose your wallet or it could get swiped. This one is a little worse since typically, your wallet has your driver's license in it. That opens up more opportunity for a clever thief to wreak havoc in your world. They now have your name, address, date of birth and maybe your social security number (depending on what you have in your wallet). If that's the case, game on! You could be buying jet skis and limo rides for people all over the world! That would be a serious bummer so, keep those wallets safe and do what my mother told me to do, memorize your social security number, then put the card someplace safe.

I should relate a story about losing my wallet when I was in law school. About a thousand years ago, I went to the circus with a friend of mine and I dropped my wallet while contemplating all the possible bar exam questions and liability issue spotting. (Fun stuff like, "I wonder what kind of waiver the guy riding the motorcycle in the cage had to sign?") A law student at a circus is like an indoor dog finally getting to ride in the car with its head sticking out of the window. Stupidly, I had everything in that wallet, including my social security card.

A very nice older man called me (yep, even my phone number was in it), and said, “You lost your wallet, I have it and you can come by my house and get it.” I was so grateful! I grabbed a friend who knew the area and immediately went to his house and got the wallet. He was a very kind, older gentleman who was probably someone’s grandfather and who did the right thing. That man still has my thanks, to this day. He also said to me, “You know, you have too many things in that wallet.” He was right! I hope he knows that he has my thanks for treating me like he would his own granddaughter and giving me some good counsel. I’m embarrassed to say that I was so overwhelmed with angst at losing my wallet that I forgot to write down his name and I can’t recall if I sent him a thank you card. I hope I did. What a class act! Thanks wherever you are. I haven’t forgotten you!

The third, and most unfortunate way identity theft happens is when someone you know steals it. That just plain stinks. I’ve seen it time and time again, though. You have someone in your life who, when your back is turned, sees an opportunity to lift your wallet, take your mail or checks, etc. This happens a lot with senior citizens who have adult children that take out credit cards in their name and crank them up to the limit. The next thing you know, they're getting sued and about to get a judgment lien on their home which, they've worked their whole life to pay off and is their only real asset, since they're on a fixed income. I've seen John Doe get his brother Jeff Doe's driver's license. John then proceeds to go out and get a DWI. The next thing you know, Jeff is out driving one day and gets pulled over for driving without a valid license. A month later, Jeff is standing in court scratching his head saying, "How in the world did this happen?"

I hate to say it, but you do need to keep an eye on your important documents if you have others in your household. I really think you will know if this advice applies to you but, here are a few things to remember in the meantime. Keep your documents in a lock box, keep your wallet safe and make sure you check your mail every day. If you pay your bills with checks, don't leave them in the mailbox over night. Make sure you put them out just before the mailman comes. Invest in a shredder, and then use it. Shred credit card solicitations, loan solicitations and anything else you don't want a thief to get his hands on.

If your identity gets stolen, immediately call the local sheriff or police and file a police report. Credit card companies and banks will usually expect a copy of it before they take any action on a debt, withdrawal or charge resulting from identity theft. If you see something questionable, act on it immediately. Most of the time, your responsibility for the charge or withdrawal will be limited if you act on it quickly enough. There are specific rules that require each of the CRAs to put credit freezes on your credit reports if you are a victim of identity theft. Contact them immediately and report it as soon as it happens. You should also contact your state attorney general. They might have some resources, like a credit freeze, that you can use to help you out with your situation.

Here are a few last suggestions that can help avoid identity theft. Keep your important documents in a fireproof lockbox, you can get one for less than $100. If you don't have one, get one immediately. Check your mail everyday. If you see something on a statement that is questionable, report it to the company who issued the statement immediately. The longer you wait, the more likely you will be held responsible for paying the charge. Finally, if your identity is stolen, contact your bank, credit card companies, local police or sheriff and all 3 nationwide CRAs. They can help you freeze your credit and minimize the damage to your credit resulting from your identity being stolen.

Epilogue

Well, there you have it! Years of personal experience, and 12 years of bankruptcy experience, crammed down into an easy to read book about how to get your financial situation under control. I really do believe that if I can do it, anyone can. Now, I do think it's important to repeat the most important piece of information in this book, and here it is: The secret to money management is, there is no secret ... you just have to do it! And you can start at any age. Take Colonel Sanders, for example. I'm pretty sure that everyone in the free world knows who he is. He was born in 1890 and in 1952, when he was 62, he hit on the idea of selling restaurant franchises for his fried chicken business. What most people don't know is that he didn't start frying chicken until the 1930s, when he was well into his 40s. He sold fried chicken out of his little restaurant for 20 years or so. Before that, he had lots of different jobs and failed at several businesses. He sold Kentucky Fried Chicken in 1964 for a boatload of money. He was 74. So remember this, if the Colonel can turn a piece of fried chicken into millions after spending most of his life failing and failing all over again, you can get your money under control. Anything is possible.

Appendix A – Four Question Flowchart

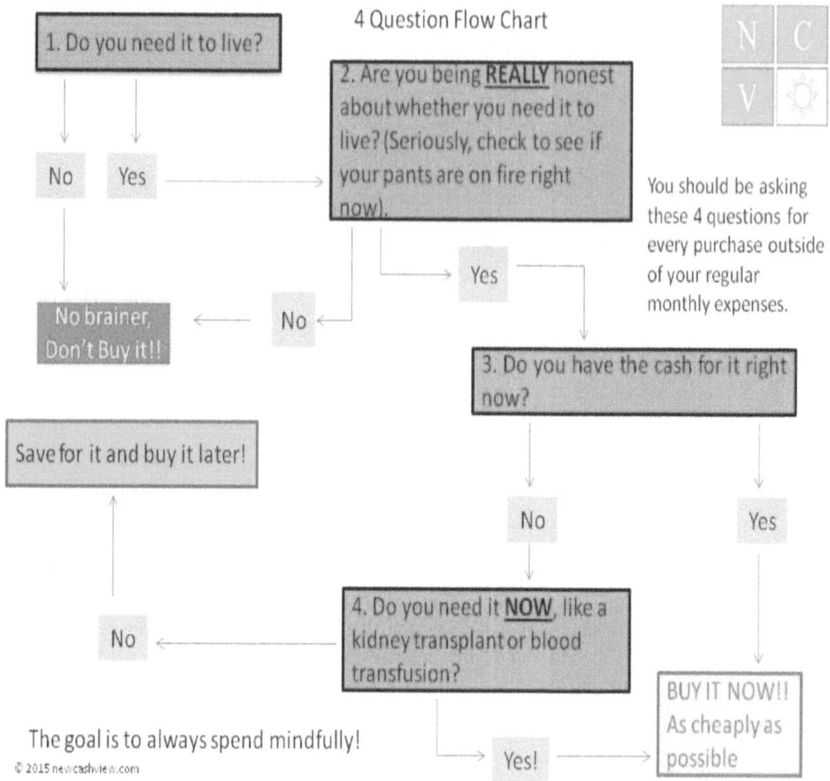

Appendix B – FTC Sample Dispute Letter – To The CRA

Note, this sample has been taken directly from the Federal Trade Commission website.

Sample Letter for Disputing Errors on Your Credit Report

Vea esta página en español

Use this sample to draft a letter disputing errors on your credit report.

Your letter should clearly identify each item in your report you dispute, state the facts and explain why you dispute the information, and request that it be removed or corrected. You may want to enclose a copy of your report with the items in question circled.

Send your letter by certified mail, "return receipt requested," so you can document what the credit reporting company received. Remember to include copies of the applicable enclosures and save copies for your files.

Related Items

- Disputing Errors on Credit Reports
- Free Credit Reports
- Credit Scores
- Credit Repair: How to Help Yourself

[Your Name]
[Your Address]
[Your City, State, Zip Code]

[Date]

Complaint Department
[Company Name]
[Street Address]
[City, State, Zip Code]

Dear Sir or Madam:

I am writing to dispute the following information in my file. I have circled the items I dispute on the attached copy of the report I received.

This item **[identify item(s) disputed by name of source, such as creditors or tax court, and identify type of item, such as credit account, judgment, etc.]** is **[inaccurate or incomplete]** because **[describe what is inaccurate or incomplete and why]**. I am requesting that the item be removed **[or request another specific change]** to correct the information.

Enclosed are copies of **[use this sentence if applicable and describe any enclosed documentation, such as payment records and court documents]** supporting my position. Please reinvestigate this **[these]** matter**[s]** and **[delete or correct]** the disputed item**[s]** as soon as possible.

Sincerely,
Your name

Enclosures: **[List what you are enclosing.]**

Appendix C – 5 Day Consumer Debt Verification Letter

Your Name Date

Your Address

Your City, State, Zip

Creditor

Creditor Address

Creditor City, State, Zip

Re: Account Number: ____________________

Dear Account Manager:

I have been contacted by your collections department on (insert date here), regarding the debt that you claim I owe and having the account number listed above.

I am writing to notify you that pursuant to 15 U.S.C. 1692g of the Fair Debt Collections Practices Act that I am formally requesting that you provide validation of this debt within 5 days from the date of (insert initial contact date here).

Please note that I will pursue all legal remedies available to me should you fail to respond within verification of the debt accordingly.

I appreciate your prompt attention to this matter.

Sincerely,

Joe Consumer

Encls.

Appendix D – FDCPA 30 Day Consumer Dispute Letter

Your Name   Date

Your Address

Your City, State, Zip

Creditor Name

Creditor Address

Creditor City, State, Zip

Re: Account Number: ____________________

Dear Account Manager:

I am writing to notify you that pursuant to 15 U.S.C. 1692g of the Fair Debt Collections Practices Act that I am formally disputing the debt assigned to my name and having the account number listed above. I am disputing it because … (enter reason for dispute here), and I have enclosed copies of the supporting documentation herewith, (that would be proof of payment, or etc.). Please respond within 30 days from the date of this letter with either verification of the debt and/or judgment, (whichever is appropriate), and proof that the debt is still outstanding. Also, you are legally required to forward the name of the original creditor if the debt did not originate with you.

If you complete your investigation and find that the debt is no longer outstanding, please correct or remove and/or withdraw the negative entries or information that corresponds with this debt from my credit report with (Equifax, Experian or Transunion, whichever CRA has the negative information listed) and notify all other appropriate agencies as required by law.

Further, please note that you must cease and desist all collection activity on this debt pending the investigation thereof pursuant to the Fair Debt Collections Practices Act. I will pursue all legal remedies available to me should you continue to attempt to collect the debt for the subsequent 30 days or fail to respond within 30 days from the date of this letter with the results of your inquiry.

I appreciate your prompt attention to this matter.

Sincerely,

Joe Consumer

Encls.

Appendix E - Printable Budget Sheet*

Income	$
Total salaries	$
Income from rental property you own	$
Investment/dividend income	$
Other source of income (child support, government assistance, etc.)	$
TOTAL INCOME	$
Expenses	
Mortgage payment or rent on primary residence	$
HOA dues	$
Homeowner's/renters insurance	$
Gas/heating fuel	$
Electric	$
Water	$
Trash	$
Telephone (landline and cell)	$
Cable/satellite/Internet	$
Home maintenance/repairs	$
Car payment	$
Car insurance	$
Gas/oil	$
Repairs	$
Tolls/parking/public transport	$
Groceries	$
School lunches	$
Restaurants/alcohol	$
Medical bills	$
Dental bills	$
Medical/dental insurance premiums	$
Prescriptions	$
Life insurance	$
Disability/long term care insurance premiums	$

Child support	$
Tuition	$
Child care	$
School/activities/hobbies/sports	$
Clothing/laundry/dry cleaning	$
Personal grooming	$
Household items	$
Pet expenses	$
Credit cards/unsecured & student loan payments	$
Investment contributions	$
Entertainment	$
TOTAL EXPENSES	$
Income - Expenses = NET INCOME	$

*Can be downloaded at newcashview.com!

Resources

Fair Credit Reporting Act. 15 U.S.C. §1681

-It also incorporates the Fair and Accurate Credit Transactions Act, 2003. (Requires 1 free annual credit report per national CRA; Has additional rules for ID theft).

Fair Debt Collection Practices Act. 15 U.S.C. §1692

- Contact the Federal Trade Commission to report violations of the Fair Debt Collections Practices Act.

www.ftc.gov or 1-877-FTC-HELP (1-877-382-4357)

www.newcashview.com

www.nfcc.org

Nationwide Credit Reporting Agencies

www.transunion.com

www.experian.com

www.equifax.com

www.annualcreditreport.com (Beware of other websites posing as this one!! You should never be asked to input a credit card number to get your credit reports.) The official site looks like this:

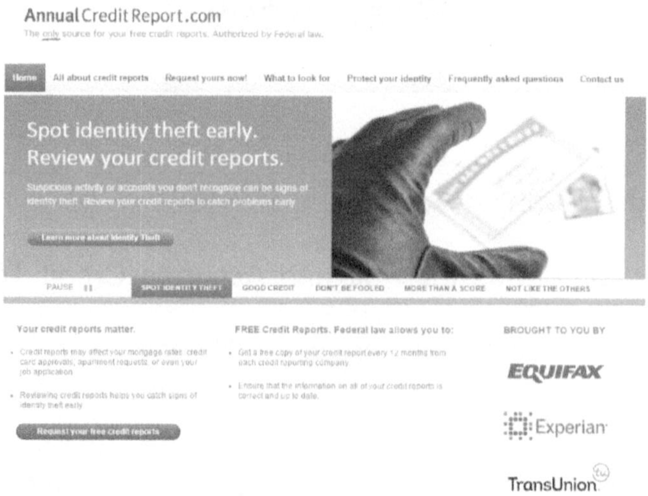

AnnualCreditReport.com
The only source for your free credit reports. Authorized by Federal law.
Home
All about credit reports
Request yours now!
What to look for
Protect your identity
Frequently asked questions
Contact us
Spot identity theft early.
Review your credit reports.
Suspicious activity or accounts you don't recognize can be signs of identity theft. Review your credit reports to catch problems early
Learn more about Identity Theft
PAUSE
SPOT IDENTITY THEFT
GOOD CREDIT
DON'T BE FOOLED
MORE THAN A SCORE
NOT LIKE THE OTHERS
Your credit reports matter.
Credit reports may affect your mortgage rates, credit card approvals, apartment requests, or even your job application
Reviewing credit reports helps you catch signs of identity theft early
Request your free credit reports
FREE Credit Reports. Federal law allows you to:
Get a free copy of your credit report every 12 months from each credit reporting company
Ensure that the information on all of your credit reports is correct and up to date.
BROUGHT TO YOU BY
EQUIFAX
Experian
TransUnion

Made in United States
Cleveland, OH
18 October 2026

46341969R00084